Always a welcome the glove compartment history of the motorway service area

David Lawrence

Between Books

Foreword by Jonathan Glancey

Architecture is the three-dimensional framework of our lives. No. Let me try that again. Buildings are the three-dimensional framework of our lives. There's long been a kind of class distinction between Architecture, which takes a capital A, and buildings. To an extent this makes sense. Architecture is building as Art, as in Salisbury Cathedral, St Paul's, the Chrysler Building, the new Guggenheim Museum in Bilbao. Buildings are no more and no less than the structures we need to cater for one function or the other: as with motorway service stations they do not need to be Art. Or they certainly aren't Art and have little or no aspiration to be so.

And yet, on a daily basis we encounter Architecture far less than we do buildings like motorway service stations. We might catch a glimpse of the spire of Salisbury Cathedral from the snarling elevated ring road that snakes around the Wiltshire city its skypiercing spire adorns, yet in our rush to get from A to B by car, we are more likely to spend a furtively stolen 30-minutes inside a roadside Little Chef or Happy Eater than we are in the meditative nave of a medieval cathedral. Even if we do decide to divert from an urban ring-road and find a parking space close to a cathedral, we are as likely to spend as much time in its chintzy tea-room as we are inside its cavernous nave. And yet whilst much is written about cathedrals, little is ever committed to print about roadside diners, and in particular those staggeringly busy and utterly fascinating motorway service stations that serve more meals to more people than probably any other form of eaterie. These are places for cars to refresh themselves too, on supertanker loads of oil and petrol.

As a nation of road users, we swarm to these curiously artless places. Their design appears to be, for better or worse, entirely free from the hands of the kind of architects who design the smart new restaurants, cafes and bars that steal pages of Sunday supplements and dominate design and decor magazines. We really ought to know more about motorway buildings, of their ambitions, their designers and their special, if ineffably banal place in our daily lives. In this book, David Lawrence is our guide, and a very good guide because his research is thorough and enquiring, his tone measured, yet his style lively and driven through with intelligent rather than patronising humour. It would be very easy to take the micky when writing about Britain's motorway service areas. Lawrence refuses to do this and is instead the kind of guide who makes such all too often crass places as utterly absorbing as in fact they really are.

Jonathan Glancey
Architecture and Design Editor, The Guardian

3

'When the first English road was built, the first English inn was born . . . it serves us all, whatever our rank.'[1]

Contents

Where to?

On the motorway, we can go anywhere. It is its own world, its own half-life of local radio reports, dislocated names on signs, its own largely monotonous landscape. And it has its own buildings. One summer day, travelling between Manchester and Liverpool on M62, I encountered two strange green roofs in the otherwise unremarkable terrain. What were they for? Who had designed them? Why were they an unusual shape? Arrival was altogether another experience: an apron of tarmac in which the buildings seemed diminished. Throngs of cars, coaches and people. Queues for food, noise and lights in the amusement arcade, the toilets. And who hasn't stopped on the motorway for refreshment, to get the children to a loo, to shake the road out of your legs or buy a present that was forgotten until after we left home?

Motorways are the trunk routes of the road network, unavoidable conduits along which millions of us travel for work or leisure. Parts of this travel experience are the motorway service areas, those much-maligned outposts once representative of Englishness at its most basic. Since the early 1950s, when the newly motorised masses joined the throngs of private hire coaches travelling from city to country, or just participated in the pastime of 'going for a drive', the culture of the motorway service area has been linked with that of the lorry driver, the family saloon car, and the seaside.

I knew that in the phrase 'North of Watford Gap', British folklore had incorp-orated a vision of that territory supposedly beyond civilisation. A look at names proposed for service areas - Newport Pagnell, Farthing Corner, Leicester Forest East, Clacket Lane - suggested a peculiar link between the tarmac ribbon just four decades old, and an ancient land.

Granada, *Fortes' Motorchef*, and the *Blue Boar* conjure up reminiscences of the road. Or maybe we just remember the weird decor of a stop on M6. Most claim the service area to be prosaic, a suburb in the country. But photography, films, literature, and pop songs feature the service area for the very reason that it *is* a place with distinctive or memorable qualities. I was curious about these brief interludes of activity, these oddly schemed spaces, and apparent communities; the feeling of being somewhere else, strange and isolated. Were they oases of rest and refreshment, entertainment venues, or just necessary journey breaks which had only to be endured?

Until now, no one has really looked at the history and development of motorway service areas, or their place in mass culture and architecture. I went looking, and travelled eight thousand miles over weekends and holidays. Everyone I met had something to say, but it seemed nobody had stopped to listen. There were few chance encounters, far too many fried breakfasts, and my friends think I'm a bit more strange than before. Here's what I found while I was out there. I have added postcards and ephemera to the pictures taken by other people, and with the history I have included tales from the motorway - stories people have told me from their times at the roadside. And would a history of motorway service areas be complete without some mementoes of the trip: battered road maps, sugar packets, stolen cutlery?

From tea and a pork pie in 1965, to hand made chocolates, socks and own-brand fragrances today, a lot of history has been condensed into forty years. Before you accelerate past to the next junction, or reach for the crisps, why not investigate this fascinating other world?

This has been a journey in a new direction for me. My deepest thanks go to Emilie Harrak, Asha Quinn and Alison Austin, for their perseverance and good navigation when I repeatedly tried to turn the map upside down. I want to acknowledge the support given to the early stages of this research by English Heritage; to Elain Harwood I offer much gratitude for the initial impetus to start this project, and for her critical reading of the text. Elain, I won't forget standing in the rain in the middle of M6 to get that photograph of Hilton Park. Without Russ Craig this work would have been much the less; he allowed me access to his archive material and provided many of the photographs used in this book. But for me it is his affectionate recollection of the roadside café seen glowing in the night that reaffirmed my intention to complete this work. I want also to thank Jonathan Glancey for contributing the foreword, and for continuing to vigorously champion the cause of all transport forms. I am grateful to Brian Gatensbury, former managing director of Granada Motorway Services, for checking facts in the draft. This publication grew out of my ongoing research work at the University of Westminster. I would like to record the support and supervision given by Tanis Hinchcliffe and Marion Roberts, and to thank Michael Browne, Richard Difford, Mike Fisher, David Greene, Andrew Peckham and Peter White. At Kingston University my friends and colleagues have made available a place to write - my thanks to Professor Peter Jacob, Helen Iball and Sue-Ann Lee, and everyone at Knights Park Library. Peter Bale and Jonathan Newey at Lamport Gilbert, and Jim Whiting of Capital Transport Publishing have advised and assisted with all aspects of this book's production. Granada Road Services have never failed to be generous in their assistance to this research. For the team at Toddington - Maurice Kelly, Maggie Mayhew, Sophie Cullen, Heather Eilbeck, Karen Head, Suzanne Hedges, Karin Montgomery, Tony Raven and Jenny Smith, and for everyone out at the sites, a very big thank you. RoadChef assisted generously; the team includes Tim Ingram Hill, Tony Cooper,

Tom Flanagan, Sue Hawkins, Ernie McVay and Rosemary Sologub. At Nikko Europe plc I would like to thank Mark Clarke, Simon Oakland and Brian Berry. Welcome Break gave full co-operation to my documenting the history of their motorway sites, and shared their vision of future developments; my gratitude goes to Steve Franklin, Peter Javes, Paul Johnson and Robin Turner. Westmorland Motorway Services contributed Lakeland hospitality and a refreshing view of the subject: thank you to John Dunning, Sarah Dunning, Michael Bult, Stephanie Boulton and Elaine Clark. At First Motorway Services, I want to thank Rob Millar, Noel Richards and Nick Palminzi. Michael Boyle and Malcolm Young, formerly of service area operators Ross Group, added unique insights into the early history of the industry. I would also like thank the following individuals and organisations: Alan Abrahams, T.P.Bennett & Partners, BDA Design: Issy Spektor, Niall Buchanan, Richard Burnett, Ian Burman, Pat Campbell, Roy Corby, David 'Strum' Craig, Dan Films: Julie Baines, Jenny Day, Bill Finch, Penny Metal, Patrick Garnett, Paul Graham, Anna Greenhow, Michael Guthrie, Patrick Gwynne, Derek Hedges, Ian Hodgson, Hook Whitehead Associates: Henry Hook/David Whitehead, Phil Hubbard, imagecare.com, Impact Design & Marketing: Paul Bryant, Christine and Colin Jefferson, Shelley Lawrence, Brian Leather, Janette and Campbell McCutcheon, Ella McGeever, Gerry Marsden, Mason-Williams: Andrew Leatham and Denise Dawson, Tony Munn, Eric Neve, Bev Nutt, Maggie O'Neill, Martin Parr, Shirley Pow, Albie Smosarski, Stephen Rosenberg, Robin Soper, Frederick Steyn, Malcolm Stockton, Lucy Strathon, Simon Suckling, Terence Conran Limited: Sir Terence Conran/Jamie Abbott, Irene Todd, U.K. Sucrologists Club: Beryl Laishley/Pam Miller/Norman Wordsworth, J. Ward Associates: Rory McCabe, Dennis Watson, Dave Wickens and Sharon Zukin.

David Lawrence, M6   November 1999

⬤ 01 Setting off

Service at the roadside

Until the 1930s the British filling station was often a group of petrol pumps thrown up at the roadside, with a building roughly adapted for its new use. A blacksmith or mechanic could accomplish necessary vehicle repairs. Safety concerns gradually saw relocation of the pumps to a pull-in off the road. Organised as a forecourt and service station, this was provided with purpose-built structures for cash handling, some equipment sales, and vehicle maintenance. Refreshments were few, travellers resorting to coaching inns, hotels and roadhouses where they could obtain relief and participate in the pleasures of staged journey-making: food, alcohol and a bed for the night. Outside urban areas transport cafés and truck driver rest-stop dormitories served lorry drivers and motorists.

A new road

At the beginning of motor car use in this country, there were few long distances that could be covered easily by road, and many routes were little more than cart tracks. During the 1920s and 1930s a national road network was realised. In building express motor roads, Britain finally began to catch up with Germany, Italy and the United States in the 1950s. Post-war reconstruction and

Left: Photographer Paul Graham traversed the A1 Great North Road several times during 1981 and 1982 to document the life he found at the side of Britain's former main north-south artery. Like Route 66 in America, the A1 was a decaying reminder of road travel in pre-motorway Britain, and on its verges remained establishments set up by enterprising individuals to serve motorists and lorry drivers. This is 'Mac's Café, Alconbury, Cambridgeshire, April 1981.'

Top: Old English roadside inn.
Above: Pre-motorway service on A74 near Crawford, Scotland.

Right: Mass exodus from town to holiday camp in the summer months added to the number of leisure activities that could be enjoyed using road transport.
Above right: 1960 scheme for a prototype service area, by architects Leonard Manasseh & Partners in response to criticisms of Watford Gap and Newport Pagnell. The design included a pedestrian piazza and various restaurant services.

decentralisation increased the need for new fast freight and passenger links. With railways out of favour, motor transport was seen as the key to making these connections. Motorways would relieve the 'A' class roads and divert overspill traffic from subsidiary routes. Car manufacture also provided employment for plant and manpower no longer supplying the war effort. The growth of private car ownership, commercial traffic and road-borne leisure journeys was rapid. Preston by-pass - the first section of British motorway albeit just eight miles-long - opened in December 1958, and would subsequently be part of M6. The seventy-five mile first section of the M1 'London - Birmingham motorway', followed this fragment on 2 November 1959.

Why service areas?

Prime Minister Harold Macmillan identified motorways as a key symbol of Britain's technological, cultural and economic progress. Domestic tourism was transformed by short holidays and day trips. Motorways allowed a considerable increase in the speed at which the country could be traversed. They proved to be a vital component in the new mass leisure. In line with policy on express roads abroad, the argument was put forward by government that service areas contributed to economy and road safety, as they limited the traffic using existing roads and reduced the fuel consumption of journeys off the motorway. Stopping on the motorway itself was prohibited except in an emergency, so off-road rest areas had to be offered. To feed the motorised masses, it was no longer sufficient for rest stops to be an ad-hoc assembly of transport café, filling station and a breakdown recovery service; comprehensively planned facilities were needed. Here was the potential for design that could respond to the entirely artificial landscape of the motorway itself.

Precedents abroad

Neither the government, which controlled provision of service areas, nor the operators or designers, knew much about what was needed for the motorway traveller. Any practical examples had to come from abroad, and there were opportunities to learn from, or at least imitate, installations in North America, Italy, and Germany. In the United States, the massive increase in tourism beginning after the second world war, was recognised by developers of lodgings and roadside restaurants. Like the wayside coaching inns, and hotels clustered around railroad stations, buildings appeared along the margins of the highways to accommodate the motor traveller: shops, diners, filling stations and motels. Construction of the Interstate Highway system began in 1956. These limited-access roads had rest areas without catering facilities. More sophisticated amenities

Left: Proposed restaurant and service station design for the New York State Thruway, USA, 1954. **Below:** The bridge restaurant that provided the model for early English service stations. This is Vinita on the Will Rogers Turnpike, Oklahoma, USA, 1957.

Above: 'Autogrill' at Montepulciano on the Autostrada del Sole, Italy, 1968. An imaginative and unique expression of modern architecture for travel.
Right: The red-roofed restaurant of Howard Johnsons - 'Landmark for Hungry Americans', a once ubiquitous sight that owed more to the romance of colonial history than the spirit of a new age.
Opposite: Ronco Scrivia 'Autogrill', Autostrada Milano - Genova.

were provided on State Turnpikes or toll roads built by private enterprise. Caterers such as Howard Johnson promoted their businesses by association with the new roads: modern travellers were encouraged to dine in appropriately modern establishments. Services were planned for twenty-four hour operation, and would comprise three types of catering for snacks, lunch and dining clustered around a kitchen, a lobby with gift shop, telephones and toilets, and an integral service station office. Some rest areas were built as bridges so that full refreshment facilities need not be duplicated on either side of the road. Service areas on the Italian autostrade were run by private concerns such as food producers and caterers, in partnership with oil companies. The Autostrada del Sole, begun in 1956 to link Milan and Rome, was the first Italian motorway for which fully planned amenities were provided.[2] A special society was established by the Italian government to approve building designs and arrange essential services for the sites, which were spaced at 20 to 25 mile intervals. Several catering developments were lavishly detailed as three-dimensional building-advertisements with masts and flags, to express their function and the joy of motoring. Services included vehicle repairs, supermarkets selling the operator's own food products, licensed bars and tourist information bureaux. (One architect who

travelled to northern Italy for research on behalf of Ross Group, recalls that several sites seemed to have shops selling heavy reproduction furniture.) Service stations and motels were built throughout Italy during the 1960s to attract traffic onto the new highways. Unlike early British operations, a local firm using trained staff usually operated the German autobahn *raststätte* (rest place), where catering and fuel would be supplemented by hotel accommodation for motorists.

Up to sixty

Design and production of British motorways was rooted in the post-war optimism of national regeneration and emerged at the start of an economic boom and extensive social change. The concept of leisure was restored with the Festival of Britain, beginning a decade of coffee bars, the return of pre-war seaside-style entertainment,

and imported pastimes such as ten-pin bowling. Steady employment, reasonable wages, and individual mobility enabled the rapid liberation of the working classes, and fuelled their desire and ability to consume. With the introduction of hire purchase, relatively large goods could be bought easily. Teenagers were a new phenomenon, aided by the abolition of compulsory call-up to the armed forces. Acquisition of fashionable clothes and pop music increased the public visibility of mass culture, and contributed to the dream of a society in which all classes could be equal.

The emphasis was on youth, fantasy and glamour, inspired by European and American magazine and film images, and proliferated through the medium of commercial television. Through their consumption and leisure, workers wanted to have the fantasy lifestyle for themselves. By the

Right: No particular place to go: Newport Pagnell, 1968. For teenagers, few towns had any kind of late night venue, and the service station proved to be an exciting alternative to what was often the only other 24-hour shelter - the all-night launderette.

Below right: Off to the Wye Valley. Before M4 - Sylvia Lawrence and George on the Aust-Clepstow ferry, 1958, photographed by Simon Lawrence.

mid-1960s advertising was appropriating the imagery and language of international air travel to create the 'Jet Age'. Those who by association or aspiration claimed status in this nebulous era, by visiting the right places, wearing the right clothes and, most importantly, driving at speed, felt themselves to be part of the 'jet set'. There were no speed limits on the motorways until 1965, and mass-produced saloon cars had top speeds edging towards the magic 'ton' of 100mph.

Architecture too had a role in the expression of progress and technology. New constructions such as the Humber Bridge and Post Office (now Telecom) Tower were modern wonders and attracted their own tourists. As a significant agent of equality, the motor car would need to be sustained by appropriate venues. By government determination, the service area would cater for different price levels and dining tastes within a single building. What emerged from the drawing boards of designers was an attempt to catch the essence of the age and refer to none other.

Potential service area customers were anyone and everyone who was using a motorised vehicle to get from one place to another - commercial drivers and travelling businessmen, followed by private motorists on city to city journeys. For many thousands of car-borne holidaymakers a stop at the motorway services was part of the ritual of going away; for the children a chance to have food and treats not normally allowed. At night cars and motorbikes would use the motorway for a high speed run, gathering at a service area to play pinball, drink coffee and generally hang around.

Motorway Service Area
Sir Owen & King c. 1961

Central control

The Ministry of Transport determined sites for motorway services. Promoters of motorway construction both here and abroad held the belief that the new highways would open up the countryside; Ministry policy was to site service areas 'in places where the motorway passed through pleasant rural scenery, so that their potential users might find them attractive and restful'.[3] Land for service areas was included in the main motorway purchases. Bought out of public funds, the sites were of the minimum acreage considered necessary. Initially the distance between service areas was approximately 12 miles, with every other site to be held in reserve until traffic levels warranted development. Building along the motorway itself was not permitted, and access was limited, so service areas would have to operate as self-contained entities in isolated locations.

Beyond basic utilities, primary landscaping, parking, access roads and a footbridge where necessary, the government required operators to provide every element of the service area. Signs were restricted to the control of traffic exiting the highway, filtering through the site and returning to the road. No advertising of any sort was allowed. In the filling station at least two different brands of

fuel had to be offered, but commonly operators were expected to provide separate pumps (with associated storage tanks, administration and accounting) for up to five petrol companies. A twenty-four hour catering service had to be provided. No alcohol could be sold. A separate transport café must always be included; this had to sell food at lower prices than the public dining areas and operators might go to some lengths to deter private motorists from visiting the transport facility. The government advertised for tenders on site leases; interested parties had to commit themselves to a certain sum for the buildings, a 50 year lease calculated according to the Ministry's expenditure in buying and preparing the site, and a rental based on a percentage of gross turnover. Government revenues would rise in line with operators' profits (and for a time exceeded them). Tenders were in two parts: a financial offer and a scheme for buildings. In the context of the extensively nationalised British industry of the time, this public-private operation of service areas was perhaps unique. Sources have suggested however that, had the opportunity arisen, civil servants would have divested themselves of any responsibility for motorway services much sooner than would eventually be the case.

Out on the blue roads: 1959-1969

First stops

Two service area sites were planned for immediate use on the first section of M1: Newport Pagnell and Watford Gap. Blue Boar, a family owned company which ran a café on A5 as well as several filling stations, were invited to develop the service areas in compensation for the expected loss to their existing business. (This was an exceptional circumstance as the smaller organisations were effectively excluded by the large minimum cost for buildings.) Blue Boar was originally to take on both sites: Newport Pagnell would be exclusively for cars, and Watford Gap for lorries. In the end it settled for Watford Gap and hotelier/caterer Fortes got Newport Pagnell.

Technically Watford Gap was the first service area in the country, opened on the same day as motorway M1 - 2 November 1959. Completion of full catering facilities was delayed and the cafés not in use until 12 September 1960, almost a month after Newport Pagnell began trading. In the meantime Blue Boar had to purchase some garden sheds from which to sell sandwiches. Motorway services were sufficiently novel to attract some interest: architect F. H. Carter appeared on television 'explaining how the service station worked, how you left the motorway and returned to it safely, and how you linked·

Gerry Marsden, of the pop group Gerry and the Pacemakers, told me that there was only the M1 in the early days of touring. The Blue Boar at Watford Gap provided 'a quick stop and a quick nosh' on the way home after a gig and 'a bit of a giggle if another group showed up'.

A now-defunct operator claimed "the first motorways were boring – they didn't need any design."

Top: Newport Pagnell, 1960.
Above: The undistinguished sheds and parking areas of the original Watford Gap, 1960.
Opposite page: Summer crowds at Newport Pagnell, 1968.

One of the first bridge restaurants - Charnock Richard, 1962.

Keele, 1968. To cope with the unexpectedly large numbers of people crowding into service stations, kiosks were opened to sell food that could be eaten in the car or picnic area.

the opposite sides of the road'.[4] Watford Gap settled down to regular trade from commercial drivers whose expectations were predictable and apparently less likely to result in complaints about levels of service. Blue Boar may not have expanded their motorway business beyond Watford Gap for almost two decades, but they gained a particular reputation. A story has it that the service station was so popular with musicians, guitarist Jimi Hendrix thought Blue Boar was the name of a London nightclub.

Newport Pagnell (opened 15 August 1960) was let to Motorway Services Ltd. - a joint venture between Forte & Co. and Blue Star Petroleum. Fortes eagerly grasped a new opportunity for expansion of their catering activities on a national scale: within a year they would announce plans for a chain of motels with restaurants and filling stations. Service areas became part of Fortes' Popular Catering division, which comprised several restaurants, Kardomah coffee houses and Quality Inns. For many years brothers Harry and Ray Dowcett vigorously managed Fortes' motorway activities from their seat of empire at Newport Pagnell. Under the Dowcetts, staff loyalty was total, but profits were given precedence over design. In 1969 Fortes' motorways operation was split and this regime lost full hold.[5]

Bridge buildings

Designers planning double-sided sites (upon which the Ministry insisted) had the difficulty of determining an overall treatment that included bisection by the motorway. At Watford Gap the issue was avoided by having separate, duplicated buildings; Newport Pagnell included a built-in footbridge. In 1957, five bridge restaurants were built on the United States' Illinois Tristate and Northwest Tollway system (see page 15). Visiting British Minister of Transport Ernest Marples admired these services, and put them forward as a pattern for future service area developments in this country. It was believed that people were thrilled by the spectacle of speeding vehicles, and anything the designer could do to bring customers into proximity with the road was encouraged.[6]

Fortes added two more sites at Keele and Charnock Richard on M6 in 1963, and began to use the trading name 'Motorchef' for their motorway operations. In these schemes Fortes tried to learn from the experience of overcrowding at Newport Pagnell. Buildings were bigger, more streamlined, but still made of prefabricated parts. The interiors were something else altogether, as architect Terence Verity had been chief art director to Associated British Cinemas. A description of Keele reveals the

Of the three catering facilities once provided at service areas, the most sophisticated was the Grill and Griddle. Styled on the steakhouse restaurant and clearly influenced by American practice, it aimed to serve a relatively upmarket meal to the commercial traveller dining on an expense account. This is Charnock Richard.

Taking a cue from air travel, some early service stations
had uniformed stewardesses to welcome motorists.

Left: Farthing Corner, 1962, in original form with open bridge-terrace and commemorative map under the canopy. For luxury dining the restaurant served smoked salmon and Whitstable oysters.
Below: Knutsford 'Motorport'. Here all motorist services were fitted into the bridge itself.

extent to which the designers were influenced by American coffee bar culture: pastel colours and plastic. In the bridge area, walls were lined in wood below a bright blue ceiling and timber mock roof beams. Perspex screens dividing dining areas featured a design of brilliantly coloured wheels. Mexican pink was selected for the foyer ceiling, and in the adjoining snack bar the colour scheme included sienna gold, Chinese yellow and light sand. Counters in the snack bar took the form of horseshoes - as used in U.S. diners - and were covered in fresco blue Formica. Even the transport cafés had architect-designed pierced wood partitions. Service area shops were then limited in size, and were not self-service. Provision of other diversionary elements such as weighing machines and one-arm bandits was clearly an afterthought, with the units being crowded into any available piece of foyer space.

Top Rank Motor Inns, an off-shoot of the J. Arthur Rank media and entertainment organisation, opened 'Motorports' at Farthing Corner (now Medway), M2, and Knutsford, M6, in 1963. These schemes were also of the bridge type, with a structure over the motorway flanked at each end by single storey buildings. Farthing Corner perhaps emphasises the fascination with passing traffic: pavilions on either side of the road linked by an open bridge to be used as a dining terrace in good weather.

At Farthing Corner I met Alan, the man with the largest collection of motorway postcards in Britain. Two full albums transported me to pristine 'sixties buildings and themed cafeterias which welcomed motorists under technicolour skies in long gone dreams of the future.

Speeding cars were seen as an appropriate backdrop to motorway dining. One of Terence Conran's first restaurants gave guests uninterrupted views of M1 at Leicester Forest East.

One night a few weeks after opening, a gang of motorcyclists escorted a lorry up to Leicester Forest East, scared the staff into hiding, and stole all the furniture from the restaurants.

Fresh fish at Leicester Forest East

As more motorways were started, several companies moved in to compete for their share of the catering trade. Ross Group diversified from fishing and frozen food production when they opened what was then the most northerly service area on M1 at Leicester Forest East in 1966. This would be the last of the bridge restaurants. It was the most sophisticated in design - a turquoise slab of building hovering over the highway, with sheer glass staircases and cantilevered balconies at either end, and a free-standing tower that served as chimney enclosure and landmark. On the bridge the catering units were arranged so that each kitchen serviced a café at the bridge ends and either the grill or 'deluxe' restaurant in the central section. A public corridor ran the full length of the bridge, and cafés had access to the balconies in good weather. Separate blocks set east and west of the main bridge amenity buildings contained transport cafés.

Terence Conran's design company styled the 'Captain's Table' restaurant at Leicester Forest East. Besides the cool quality of furniture and table accoutrements, waiters were dressed as captains and waitresses as sailors. Ross found that to increase profitability it had to cater to a wider audience than just the motorway traveller. Customers could enjoy an *à la carte* menu supplied by Ross's own fishing fleet, and speciality weeks when 'food from overseas' would be served. This venue was one of the few motorway restaurants to draw a regular trade from the locality, and the only service area to be awarded a five star rating by the Automobile Association, who also claimed it to be the most expensive at which to dine.[7] *Interior Design* magazine wrote enthusiastically of Leicester Forest East in 1970: 'from the windows the customers see the perspective of the road vanishing into the distance. In such interiors there is no need to bar exterior noise; nor is crowding to be decried - these are necessary elements in providing the right mood and atmosphere'.[8] The 'Captain's Table' (and other motorway grill rooms) did not last long. Motorists just did not want to pay the premium prices or delay their journeys with leisurely meals.

Bridge buildings were most suitable when the majority of the site was flat. Construction and operation costs were greater due to the extra storey, and the stairs deterred or prevented some individuals from reaching the eating areas. Kitchens were duplicated, incurring further expense, although one set of catering facilities

Previous spread, left: Farthing Corner, 1964; **right:** Early fast food stall at Knutsford, 1968.

could be closed whilst maintaining the twenty-four hour service in the other. This arrangement did not provide well for future extension. By its very nature the bridge would be costly to expand widthways, and there was a limit to the possible width before the bridge reached the Ministry of Transport's definition of a tunnel, a feature not permitted unless a necessity of topography. Any addition to the bridge at either end was also more distant from the kitchens, increasing staff time. In 1972 the *Architectural Review* offered a criticism of the bridge buildings: 'the traditional service station is like a motorised railway station and stands obtrusively across the Way…[like] the children of the thoughtless architecture of the quick buck'.[9] The bridge restaurant made no allowance for an escape from the motorway; the user remained in the environment of vehicles and the super-human scale of the road. As advertisements they were failures too: by the time drivers saw the bridge it was too late to turn off. Whilst these few service stations have become icons of British motorway

history, they are no longer considered suitable by the operators. One site at least has prompted a vision of demolition and redevelopment, but the bridge substructure is still owned by the government and, for the purposes of accounting, clearance costs would be prohibitive.

Toddington

Granada Group, creators of soap opera *Coronation Street*, and operators of many cinemas and bingo halls, extended their entertainment empire by joining the competition for motorway catering in 1965, with Toddington on M1. This site housed extensive facilities in two double-storey buildings, supplemented by separate shops and cafés. Two further sites opened in almost as many years at Frankley (M5, 1966) and Heston (M4, 1968). When Granada's motorway division was set up it shared accounting facilities with the theatres' operation, and was based in London. Brian Gatensbury (managing director of Granada Motorway Services from 1970 to 1991), removed it first to Heston,

CHILDREN'S MENU

COPPER GRILL

Orange Juice 1/-
Tomato Soup or Soup of the Day 1/-
Fish Fingers with Fried Potatoes 2/6
Fillet of Plaice (Fried or Grilled)
with Fried Potatoes 5/-
Egg with Fried Potatoes 2/6
Hamburger with Creamed or Fried Potatoes 2/6
Sausages with Creamed or Fried Potatoes 3/-
Breast of Chicken, Peas and Creamed Potatoes 5/-
Egg Salad 3/6
Fruit Cocktail with Ice Cream 2/6
Ice Cream with Chocolate Sauce 1/-
Ice Cream 9d.
Orange or Lemon Squash 1/-
Milk 1/-
Coca-Cola 1/-

GRANADA MOTORWAY SERVICE M1 TODDINGTON

Above left: Foyer of Toddington (northbound) with stairs up to the grill room. Note the clusters of coloured fibreglass light shades and striped wall decoration. There were strict limits on the number of amusement machines which could be installed.

Above: Separate shop unit, Toddington (northbound), 1968.

and finally to Toddington, as he felt that the management would best understand the business if they were 'living on the motorway'. Special leaflets were issued to direct motorists around the services, and the original team of security staff were dressed with Robin Hood-style hats.

To coddle the motorway-stained traveller [10]

Top Rank Motor Inns opened Motorports at Forton, Lancashire, and Hilton Park in north Birmingham, both on M6. Planning of Forton commenced in 1963, and Hilton Park the following year; Forton came into use in 1965. At this time there were so few service areas, indeed so little motorway, that each new design was potentially an opportunity for advertisement and business generation, with a relatively generous budget to support it. Top Rank invested heavily in both sites. At Forton, which was within reasonable driving distance of Preston and Blackpool, the operator wanted to increase profits by enticing customers for dining and recreation, in addition to providing a service for travellers between England and Scotland. The main attraction was a 65-foot high tower with restaurant. Towers were a popular symbol of progressive architecture during this period, and constructed in many cities. Forton is also reminiscent of an airport control tower, and therefore carried positive associations with air travel - the most exclusive form of transport.

Above right: For motorists not wishing to take a lift up the observation tower at Forton, banks of automatic machines near the car park dispensed food and drink.
Right: View north from the Forton tower restaurant, 1968. Above this level was an open 'sun deck' with distant sight of the Pennines and Blackpool Tower.
Opposite page: Forton from the south.

'Diesel Lil' spent her days and nights traversing the M6 motorway, plying her trade keeping lorry drivers warm, and giving herself the occasional wash-down in a service area loo.

Left: Banks of vending machines were installed at the Motorports: 'eventually micro ovens will be installed, for "cook-it-yourself" food in 15 seconds, destroying the last vestiges of human contact'.[11]
Above and opposite page: Hilton Park.

As a variant on the tower, Hilton Park had a projecting deck restaurant on the northbound side, oversailing the lower floors. The footbridge emerged at first floor level, spanning slip roads and carriageways to link with the second storey south-bound restaurants and ground floor cafeterias. Inside the building, the grand atmosphere was emphasised by the inclusion of a 'feature stair-case', supplemented by two passenger lifts. Forton benefited from some furniture by the Italian designer Harry Bertoia, but Hilton Park had the most minimal furniture provision. Each dining area - decorated with kingfisher blue and green hessian walls and orange counter fronts - had serried rows of fixed tables and chairs, comprising no more comfort than was necessary for a twenty-minute meal stop. One magazine wrote about Hilton Park with enthusiasm, noting the toilets luxuriously furnished with foot controlled ready-mixed taps and special baby care facilities. Hilton Park was completed in 1967. Operator Top Rank had based their financial calculations on government traffic forecasts that failed to materialise due to road

diversions and drainage problems, and the service area remained closed to motorists until 1970.

The Top Rank Motorports were almost unique in the genre of motorway service area design. Using expressive forms and adventurous engineering, the designers of Forton and Hilton Park produced buildings equal to their dynamic situations, buildings that seem particularly appropriate for places that have no other locating element than the regular and apparently infinite strip of the motorway. The quick in-out nature of service means that buildings with more than one level are more expensive to operate and difficult to use - easy access being a key part of the service. Changing trends in catering and marketing concepts have seen these sites altered and extended many times; economics mean that the tower restaurant at Forton has been closed since 1989 and is now in use as offices for Granada. Hilton Park's northbound elevated restaurant currently (1999) functions as one of the few remaining motorway service area cafés; the tea tastes all the better for being served in the unfussy surroundings associated with truckers.

One regular visitor to the services at Hilton Park is 'Charlie', said to be the ghost of a worker who died on the construction site. Several staff working late or night shifts have felt a chilled presence or seen a spectral figure. Charlie seems to be harmless, but he doesn't spend much in the restaurant either.

Above left: Two large restaurants were set side by side in the single service building at Aust. Stone for construction was brought across the River Severn from the Forest of Dean; cedar boards lining the upper walls soon weathered to silver-grey, helping to blend building into sky.

Above: The 'Grand Prix Grill' at Aust, 1966.

Beside the river

After criticism of the early service areas, the government raised its expectations of new projects: the first series of designs submitted early in 1964 for Aust, M4 (now called Severn View, M48), close to the new and prestigious Severn Bridge, were rejected. Top Rank was successful in the second competition for Aust. This was the first site to be accessed from a roundabout off the motorway. Nine hundred diners could be fed at once in three catering areas within the single building. All food preparation was carried out on-site, requiring an array of kitchens and food stores that were hidden from view by placing the building in a depression of the ground. Through walls composed almost entirely of windows, customers had a panoramic view of the Severn bridge and river. I visited Aust at Easter, and found it almost empty. Below the public areas, cavernous rooms stored old neon signs, food counters, festive banners and mousetraps. The pop art mural that once gave lorry drivers a quick thrill in the transport café (see page 40) was long gone. I showed a 1966 postcard of Aust to Kevin the maintenance man. He recognised the woman in the picture as his auntie, a long-serving member of the staff. After so many years rooted in this place of temporary occupation, Kevin could date every change made to the site by events in the life of his family.

Trowell Mecca Village

'Coax us ever so slightly and we will wax lyrical about Mecca Village. We have brought into being an entirely new concept in Motorway Service Areas. We prefer to look upon Mecca Village as a place to drive TO rather than a place to drive through. An oasis on a concrete strip if you like.'[12]

In its ambitious development and exuberant promotion by Mecca Leisure Group, Trowell on M1 seems to have exemplified the mood of glamour and fantasy that infused the first half of the 1960s. Part roadside café, part B-grade film set, it offered a venue for the upwardly, and most definitely mobile, new consumers to break their journeys and banquet with their peers.

Mecca's empire included ballrooms (soon to be restyled as discotheques), ice rinks, restaurants and bars, and the Group had an eye on any new opportunities in the entertainment industry. Motorway catering looked like being a good prospect, especially as Mecca felt the existing operators were not giving it their best efforts. Michael Guthrie, who worked on the development of Trowell and has continued to bring new ideas into the service industry ever since, recalls visiting French restaurants and also being inspired by the Disney style of customer service.

Above left: Frankley (northbound), opened by Granada on M5 south of Birmingham in 1966. Motorists travelling south enjoyed the additional feature of a balcony restaurant overlooking the motorway to fields beyond. **Opposite page:** Pop Art-style collage mural in the transport restaurant at Aust, designed by Trevor Pattison 'to cheer up the lorry drivers'. It had been re-moved by the mid-1970s.

Themed interiors were popular for bars,
restaurants and other leisure sites such as holiday
camps. The architects for Trowell, which opened in
1967, designed a restrained modern building,
enclosed in glass with sleek lines like a fast car. But
Mecca wanted to cheer up the travelling public,
fashioning Trowell as a 'Village', and relating it to
the local folk hero Robin Hood. Why not forget the
motorway for a moment, and return to an ancient,
mythic England? Dining areas were named
'Sheriff's Restaurant' and 'Marian's Pantry'. The
architects had to refinish their functional interiors
in a pastiche mediaeval style. This was
accomplished by the installation of murals
depicting Hood and his merry men,[13] heavy
wooden furniture and fabric valancing fixed to
ceilings. Suits of armour, heraldic devices and a
plastic tree completed the decorations. Extra
facilities met the motorist's every need: 'village'
shops, transport drivers' clubs, over a hundred
vending machines, a coach party room, meeting
hall, a covered petwalk for the 'comfort of canine
friends', and 'for the traveller in trouble…lightning
service facilities'. Trowell proved to be very popular
with customers, but Mecca was not happy with
high rents paid to the government. The 'Village'
was sold to Granada in October 1977 and rapidly
refurbished in a contemporary style.

Left: Woodall (northbound)
- entrance in centre and main
restaurant to left of picture.
Below: Woodall (southbound)
restaurant, 1968.
Bottom: Woodall shop.

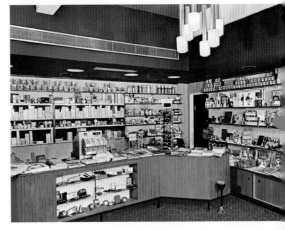

Fortes only had three motorway sites until 1968: the two bridge restaurants on M6 at Keele and Charnock Richard, and Newport Pagnell, their hub of empire. With M1 edging closer to Leeds, the Woodall site came up for tender. Roy Corby, designer of the service buildings, said that he looked around at other service areas and wanted to do something better. Woodall is remarkable for its use of different building designs on each side of the motorway, connected by a footbridge crossing at an acute angle and descending directly into the southbound block. Rather than try to enclose the different services in one big structure, varied separate forms rose above the single storey circulation spaces. Even the water tanks were made distinct by their being installed behind glazed screens. This feature gave particular emphasis to the roof of the rotunda restaurant (southbound).

Miss England flies in

Closest yet to the metropolis, and the first services to be built on M4, Granada's Heston aimed at capturing trade bound for Heathrow Airport or fuelling up for the long haul west. M4 still petered out at Maidenhead in 1968, and even when it reached Bristol and beyond in the early 1970s there were large gaps in services for motorists, so Heston was a good site to have. Granada, no strangers to showmanship with a growing television empire, made a point of letting everybody know about their third motorway site by having Jennifer Lewis, Miss England, arrive by helicopter to open the services with pop star Joe Brown.

Designed by James A. Roberts, architect for the radical redevelopment of Birmingham and Liverpool in the 1960s,[14] Heston introduced to British motorways the feature of a staggered layout, with two amenity buildings spaced some distance apart along the motorway without any physical connection between the sides. Roberts experienced difficulties persuading Granada that his two-storey, glass-fronted design was appropriate, and had further disagreement over the colour of bricks he wanted to use. Heston

was built to a much reduced specification, although the *Sunday Times* reported the extensive single-storey buildings as 'glossy restaurant complexes'.[15] Compromise is ever present in architecture, and designers do not always like to see their vision of a future building diminished by others, but here Granada may have been reasonable in letting business sense overrule the desire to be flamboyant. The catering service outshone the aesthetics of their architecture, and their profits were good. Both sides of the service area have since been entirely redeveloped following a fire and improvements to facilities.

Top: Heston, 1969.
Above: Miss England, Joe Brown and Granada's Brian Gatensbury at the opening of Heston.

For many years Heston was a venue for local youths out for a midnight drive, and latterly a rendezvous for hopeful partygoers, seeking the next telephoned instalment of directions to an illegal warehouse party that was always on a grey factory estate, somewhere out near Heathrow. I can remember a crowd for the telephone box, music and headlights round around the car park. A foray inside the building was invariably for the toilets, a Coke or hot chocolate to keep out the early morning chill.

A haven of tranquillity

For British motorway services, the sixties ended with a glamorous flourish in the shape of Scratchwood, London's first truly urban service area.[16] Fortes had noted the success of Granada's Heston, and by this time the University College London study - which found the first service area out of a city enjoyed fifty percent more trade than any other - had been published in three different, and widely available, forms. Scratchwood was also important as it was both the first stop point out of London heading north - and therefore would advertise the presence of Fortes services further up

We zipped up M1 to Scratchwood one rainy afternoon, to find it had been renamed 'London Gateway' and extensively rebuilt (for increased levels of trade), by Welcome Break. It was sad to find that the planted courtyard – Scratchwood's secret garden – once an oasis for motorists on the brink of the city, was gone: now just another part of the food court.

the motorway, and was the last opportunity for a business traveller to have refreshment before a London meeting. Fortes appear confident about this venture, and after operating sites out in the sticks, were determined to transform the disused railway yard at Hendon into an upmarket catering affair. To this end they abandoned the usual big office, any-building-you-like type architects, and went instead for the trendy Garnett, Cloughley Blakemore and Associates, who were more used to fitting-out shopping and dining dens of chrome and glass along London's hip King's Road in Chelsea. This selection is significant - firms who worked in retail and entertainment brought an

imagination to services that was much needed if motorists were to be distracted from the road even briefly. Conceived by an architect, a film designer and the man who put the 'Beachcomber Bars' in Butlins, from the outside Scratchwood has the classy look of a bank or offices built for somewhere rather more swish and temperate than north London. A colonnade of marble and granite coated concrete columns, connected to the roof beams only by fine polished steel pins, stood forward of large bronze-coloured glass windows.[17] Using 'a good measure of camp to give it a kick', the designers saw that motor references were excluded from the interior decoration. 'We were into earthy

colours like greens and browns, with orange as a bright colour highlight'.[18] In came chrome, mirrors, rosewood, apple green vinyl upholstery and a carpet designed especially for Scratchwood by Italian Baron Alexander Albrizzi, an associate of the architects. Within the building a planted central courtyard could be viewed by diners. Planning was innovative, with one kitchen for the three serveries. The *Architects' Journal* feted Scratchwood for its 'anti-motorway philosophy...[it] deliberately turns its back on traffic. It is intended as a haven of tranquillity, a soothing influence on frayed nerves, and a refuge from the stresses and irritations of motorway driving'.[19]

Charlie Bubbles (Albert Finney, in his 1968 film of the same name) is a successful writer who seems distanced from his working class origins. Accompanied by his assistant (Liza Minelli) Charlie drives a gold Rolls Royce north one night to visit his ex-wife in Manchester. They pull in to Newport Pagnell for coffee. Figures are silhouetted on the footbridge. In the deserted snack bar, in this no-man's land on the motorway, Charlie has a brief rendezvous with a glamorous old flame and her entourage.

No takers on the motorway

The first half of the 1960s could be considered a honeymoon period for motoring. Go-anywhere dreams of the late-1950s strained roads made in another age, and driving conditions became far from free and easy. Public fascination with motorways and the practice of 'motorway gazing' declined in the late 1960s, in part due to the introduction of a maximum speed limit. The first service areas were so crowded (I was amazed by just how many people there were in old pictures of these places), so successful, that companies saw only fortunes to be made. Competition for sites had become so intense that operators offered to pay rents far higher than were realistic, calculating their returns even before the new roads were finished, using flow forecasts that proved to be more than optimistic.

The interval of twenty-five miles between sites had been set by the government and was partly dictated by land acquisitions made when the motorway was planned. Infill sites at 12.5-mile intervals could be added if demand was gauged to have increased sufficiently. Due to the Ministry of Transport's ruling on monopoly, two adjacent service areas could not be leased to the same company. This precluded some savings in delivery costs, and diminished the opportunity for a greater presence on the motorway

that might have improved advertising potential - caterers were not allowed to advertise their services at the roadside. The *Sunday Times* reported in 1966 that only three out of the seven service area operators were making a profit. The *Financial Times* noted that 'after substantial losses, none of the present operators want new contracts'.[20] Woolley Edge service area, M1, advertised for operating tenders in August 1966 without success, was re-advertised in mid-1967 and still available in June 1968. Granada considered selling its motorway interests in 1968, but hung on and began to make a profit in the early 1970s.

Motorway users were a target audience for commercial activity, and catering companies were keen to take advantage of the captive trade rolling-in on the slip roads. Unfortunately the same companies wished to provide their services as economically as possible, especially as profit expectations were not being met in the face of relatively large initial investments, high turnover rents, and uncompleted road links. Because of the high original investment, on which a successful tender would depend, competition was extremely limited both at the development stage and during operation. The Ministry ban on alcohol sales - the public was never convinced by 'Wunderbar White wine' or 'Scandinavian mock-beer' - discouraged customers from an extensive meal, and the standard of food was seen to decline, aided by regular press commentary.

There was 'very little science about service area design; the Government just provided traffic forecasts...in the early days a rule of thumb was used for working out the number of toilets, café seating and other facilities'.[21] One operator remarked that Newport Pagnell was 'built on the scale of a milk bar...people in the business were shocked by the volume of trade, which they had underestimated'.[22] Caterers and designers had to hope that their schemes would function as they intended but in planning the emphasis had been on functional use only - much like airports of the day. The first service areas were unable to cope with so much traffic: 'no one had thought enough about an age of day-trippers who would want scenic enjoyment, ease of travel, food, shopping and travel information as part of the whole motorway package'.[23]

Other problems included large-scale vandalism: as the motorways were designed for long distance use rather than local communities, there was no sense of ownership or belonging. Any individual or group with destructive intentions could effect a large amount of damage within minutes and be on their way before the matter was noticed. Operators experienced massive amounts of theft. This ranged from the removal of whole frozen carcasses from the meat stores by staff on night shifts, to several thousand pounds worth of metal cutlery stolen by travellers each year. Operators then tended to take the hardened attitude that they would use the most basic building materials and furnishings, and the crudest forms of disposable plates, cups and eating implements.

The Minister steps in

As a result of criticisms aimed at service areas and their operators, in 1965 the Minister of Transport commissioned a detailed study of the industry from University College London. It was completed in February 1967, but only began to have effect in the early 1970s as projects like Heston and Woodall (both 1968) and Scratchwood (1969) were already underway. Most of the study was carried out Bev Nutt. The research was aimed at increasing the understanding of factors influencing the profitability and quality of British service areas, and looked at their design, operation and use in England, Germany, Italy and the United States.

Problems affecting service area design were many: changing population figures, increased speed of travel through better vehicle design, land use change, travel behaviour, eating habits and catering methods. An extremely wide spectrum of customers had to be catered for. Local difficulties included handling the considerable fluctuation in peak and off-peak traffic volumes without serious delay to trade or redundancy of facilities. The government's insistence on double-sided sites increased developer costs.

With no dedicated central framework for appraising planning or design, and no control over the financial offer by the operator which would effectively determine success or failure of the tender package designers of service area buildings were hardly encouraged. Bev Nutt claimed that that the symbolic form of the link or bridge was inappropriate: there was no statistical evidence whatsoever that "eye catching" developments sited over or immediately adjacent to the motorway to act as advertisements for the operators, attracted any more trade than single sided developments. He commented that 'building finishes are often quite inappropriate, flashy and far from cheap. The whole illusion of grandeur that such attitudes produce does not add to the trade'.[24] Bridge restaurants finally met their end when service stations were added to existing motorways - operators would not countenance the tens of thousands of pounds per day expected by the government to implement detours around a construction site.

A conclusion of the research report was that, without undue constraints, opportunities for service area business, and the level of custom expected, were increasing year on year with the increase of motorway traffic. Free from the proximity of competition experienced in an urban situation, the industry was becoming increasingly attractive as the various segments of motorway were joined into a useful network.

Proposals for change

The report called for flexible planning which did not rely solely on the government's traffic prediction statistics - suggesting this was the first move in thinking away from a purely economical approach to service area planning. To enable cost savings during slack periods of the twenty four hour cycle, and in low seasons of the year, it should be possible to close-off some areas within the building without affecting all services. A single, central kitchen in each amenity was most appropriate (many American Interstate diners were based on this format). To cater for refreshment provision at times of lowest demand Nutt suggested greater use of automatic vending machines as the sole providers of light snacks and drinks. Several operators tried this equipment without success - the machinery was delicate and susceptible to misuse or poor maintenance. Nutt noted that different categories of catering demanded - from transport café to waitress service restaurant - were likely to change as eating habits and lifestyles altered: any building in which these demarcations were fixed was liable to become obsolete. He anticipated that 'the only way to increase profitability was 'by persuading those that stop to spend more'.[25]

04 Ahead to the 'seventies 1970 - 1974

Off we go

The UCL report on motorway service areas call for the production of more flexible and utilitarian buildings for service stations, coincided with a sense among motorway caterers that the first series of developments had been more costly than the profits justified. Operators became aware of the need to maintain business through better facilities. One company's policy statement recognised that 'the public is becoming more discriminating and better educated...service areas are developing rapidly and the level of competition will increase'.[26] Did motorists want comfort, cheap food, clean facilities, or a thrilling recreational environment? Mostly, they just wanted toilets, tea without queues, and then a relaxing space to drink it in. But buildings are advertisements, whether they are to convey service, opulence, or refer to some kind of culture like the fast-food restaurant. Most operators relied upon the architects to advise them of what was appropriate, and continued to build service stations that drew on various themes in styling. Some were more successful than others. Oil companies were amongst the few organisations that had sufficient means to invest in service area developments, and saw that such facilities would increase their motorway fuel sales. With a useful

Ella (opposite, second from right, back row) and Shirley (centre, front row): 'It was a nice job, new, different, a flow of people going somewhere...they were going to enjoy themselves. We had specially made brown jackets and mini-skirts, and orange chiffon blouses'.

Left: Washington-Birtley, looking across the A1(M) to the village of Portobello, 1970. This is the longest motorway footbridge in Britain.

Below: An advertisement for the launch of Washington-Birtley motorway Taverna, 1970.

STEP INTO ANOTHER WORLD

TAVERNA

- EXCITING MENU INCLUDING SPECIALITY DISHES
- 24 HOURS SERVICE - 7 DAYS A WEEK
- A LUXURY RESTAURANT FOR 430 PEOPLE
- A PERFECT END TO AN EVENING OUT - VISIT THE TAVERNA ON YOUR WAY HOME

motorway system becoming a reality in the early 1970s, there were fresh opportunities to compete for new site tenders alongside the existing, and by this time somewhat disillusioned, catering operators. Accompanying the oil firms was a new generation of architects, and the desire to produce good quality buildings quickly. By the end of the sixties, concrete had proved not to be the solution to every architectural adventure, and its use was discouraged by local authority planning officers. Bridge restaurants were too costly to develop and alter, so new service stations were based on square or rectangular boxes, with hard slick exteriors of brick or cement block, and open plan interiors. Where possible, landscaping and tree planting created a barrier between the motorway and service areas.

'It's like something out of Startrek - a space fantasy!'

Esso Motor Hotels had embarked upon a pan-European motel building programme in 1963. Esso was the first of the oil companies to speculate on British service area development, seeing them as practical links for travellers between a growing chain of overnight stops. Five 'Tavernas' were planned in a brief but ambitious expansion programme for England's motorways. Washington-Birtley (A1M) opened in 1970. Leigh Delamere (M4), Birch (M62), Southwaite (M6) and Woolley Edge (M1) all opened in 1972.[27]

Motorway culture hit the north east with Washington-Birtley Taverna, a few miles south of Newcastle. Esso already had a filling station and café on the site, and got offered the service area project without having to compete against other operators. Washington-Birtley was referred to as the country's 'first robot transport café'. With a menu that offered delights such as duckling à l'orange and Coq au Vin, all food was part cooked and then placed in vending machines. Food would be accompanied by a coloured plastic token which determined the cooking time in the microwave ovens. In forty seconds a fully heated meal was ready. Ella McGeever and Shirley Pow told me that the best jobs they ever had were as uniformed hostesses (defiantly not just *waitresses*) at Washington. Trained in deportment, manicure and even how to deliver a baby, and wearing tailor-

Right: Looking more like an office or an airport than a motoring caff, southbound restaurant at Washington, with walkway above foyer. Special lamps were designed for the ceiling.

made uniforms, the ladies assisted motorists using some of the first microwaves available to the public anywhere in Britain. By all accounts the machines were temperamental. Reheated fried eggs were constantly exploding, peas jumping around on the plate, and sometimes the machines went completely wrong, reducing meals to a blackened crisp.

Washington-Birtley's layout included the innovation of slip roads beside the motorway (a common practice in Europe) which meant parking and services could be built away from the carriageway to allow for future expansion. At first, only the southbound side was fully developed; travellers in the other direction were persuaded to cross the bridge by the inducement of an 'up' escalator. Until recently, Washington was the only service area to have included this feature, which was removed some years ago because of vandalism. (Welcome Break is now installing escalators to improve access at some sites with footbridges). Motorists who did use the bridge found themselves entering the main building on an elevated walkway, with the same

feeling of grand arrival as an airport terminal. From the walkway travellers could immediately see the vending machines and there was a sense of theatre in watching activities of the diners below. (Nearby is the village of Portobello, a small settlement where many people knew each other; in the evenings it was not unusual to recognise a man entertaining someone else's wife in the service area café.) This exuberance continued in the decoration. Architect Frederick Steyn chose turquoise carpets, and gold vinyl wallpaper to create a bright shimmering strip above the foyer area. Informal partition to the dining areas was achieved by installing several hangings of collaged fabric by artist Louise Grose,[28] based on a heraldic theme representing the coats of arms of north-east civic, ecclesiastical and scholastic bodies. Air travel once again provided a model for egalitarian design: Steyn remembers that the interior layout was 'deliberately like an airport concourse, which was felt appropriate to handle people, let them mill around, decide what they wanted to do, and not be compartmentalised. The free movement was also to encourage impulse buying.'[29]

Above: Washington ladies' night out at the 'mediaeval banquet', Lumley Castle, Chester-le-Street, 1970.

"Welcome to Esso's New Motoring Service"

Esso is the first petroleum company to be awarded the entire operation of a service area by the Ministry of Transport... This new breed of motorway service area is now open at Washington, Co. Durham.

To pinpoint the exact locale: it's built on two facing sites across the new A1 (M) just south of Newcastle, so that motorists travelling either way can pull in for... well, anything. Full and fast service station facilities. First-class catering... everything from a self-service restaurant to pre-packed food you microwave cook yourself. Spotless toilet accommodation. Nappy changing rooms. Vending machines dispensing just about anything a motorist needs. 24-hour breakdown service. In fact, when you enter Esso's new Motorway Service Area, it'll feel more like walking into an airport. Everything's designed for people on the move. Everything's there for the comfort and convenience of the long-distance motorist.

Sample the Esso brand of hospitality. Drive into Esso's new Motorway Service Area next time you're near it.

24-HOUR BREAKDOWN SERVICE

VENDING MACHINES

RESTAURANT

TAVERNA

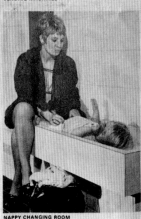

NAPPY CHANGING ROOM

AT WASHINGTON/BIRTLEY MOTORWAY SERVICE AREA

Discussing the exterior, which was originally to have been finished in pink bricks, Steyn comments that the design had 'no relation to the local area - the motorway made its own architecture'.[30]

The designers of Washington produced entirely different buildings for Woolley Edge (M1) and Birch (M62), taking inspiration from the design of Howard Johnson diners and motor inns in the United States. The sweeping red roofs carried partway down outstretched beams that characterise the Woolley Edge and Birch buildings, were seen as an appropriate response to the agricultural context; they also suggest shelter from the possibility of bad weather at this exposed location. Woolley Edge was acclaimed by the *Architectural Review* as 'surely the most spectacular site of any motorway service area in the country...the building's rather whimsical charm will be appreciated by all who use it...an *authentic* architectural experience'.[31] At Birch the roof feature was reconfigured to provide two back-to-back structures on each side of the carriageways.

Leigh Delamere (M4, which featured in the *Guinness Book of Records* for being the largest service area in Britain, at 57 acres) and Southwaite (M6) were a deliberate attempt to minimise the impact of buildings in the landscape, but still provide all the necessary facilities. Plain walls and large windows seem to confirm the temporary nature of this roadside architecture: changes would be cheap and easy to make without spoiling the visual appearance. Leigh Delamere, for a time the only rest stop on M4 between London and the Severn crossing, had virtually identical buildings on either side of the motorway. These were made distinctive by having roofs made up of twelve asymmetrical pyramids, likened by architect Christopher Dean to 'tents in the woods'.[32]

Above: Birch (M62), showing how the designers took the form of Woolley Edge and doubled it to make a larger structure.

Above: Leigh Delamere.
Above right: Southwaite.
Opposite page: Interior of Southwaite.

When the mandatory transport café gave way to the all-purpose cafeteria in the early 'seventies, truckers used to refer to some service areas as 'Plastic Jungles' – plastic cutlery, plastic crockery, plastic food.

The designers created an impression of arrival by planting an avenue of trees up to the canopied entrance, with the rather hopeful expectation that passengers would be dropped off before cars were parked.[33] Southwaite was opened for northbound travellers heading up towards the border with Scotland. Its single catering building, with walls of grey cement blocks under a lead-covered roof turned, literally, away from the motorway to offer some views into the landscape. With the Department of Transport discouraging commercial activity at service stations, Esso concentrated on selling fuel, and reportedly could not make their sites pay. The five service areas passed to Granada in 1973. All automatic vending machines were promptly removed. Southwaite was so popular

with motorists that Granada added a full amenity building in 1977 for travellers going south.

Ross gains speed

After Leicester Forest East had been operating for some years, Ross Group reconsidered their attitude to motorway services. Like other roadside restaurants and grill rooms, the Captain's Table at Leicester Forest East seems to have been an over estimation of the standards expected by British motorists, its development costs not justified by returns, and its furnishings too delicate for the heavy use. With a large national transport network linked to its frozen food business, Ross could easily run more service areas. Two schemes were won in competition: Membury (M4, opened 1972) and

Membury made reference to Scandinavian architecture and nineteenth century industrial buildings - walls of hard bricks and sharp corners laid with great precision. All diners were served in a single space separated only by screens.

Hartshead Moor (M62, opened 1973). Membury was selected because there was no competition nearby and none likely to open for some years. Ross would have preferred to build a bridge restaurant at Membury, but could not countenance the cost of traffic diversions.[34] As an alternative, both Membury and Hartshead Moor were positioned so that diners could contemplate grassy earth banks. Picking up on the theme of strong roof designs, Membury's two identical, south facing amenity buildings were set under canopies designed like rolling waves. In describing the corrugated steel surfaces which swept above diners heads, the *Architectural Review* compared the '"heavenly allusion" of the Baroque ceiling…to the brilliant design ploys of the Citroen company during their heyday'.[35] Sodium lighting played on the ceilings, illuminating the darker recesses of the serving areas and recreating some of the ambience of the motorway. An original colour scheme of blackcurrant coloured Formica tables and tangerine vinyl seats was rejected. Membury proved too grand: customers did not want to climb a ramp up to the dining areas, and space beneath the roof

required extensive heating in the winter. (Now Welcome Break has fitted an escalator that rises through a new void in the open-plan first floor to food counters and informal seating.) At the instigation of parent company Imperial Group, who felt that a direct association with motorways might not be good for their reputation, Ross Services was renamed Motoross circa 1975.

Four more for Fortes

Fortes continued steadily to build: Corley served the M1-M6 link from 1972; Fleet (M3) and Gordano (M5), were added in 1973, and Burtonwood (M62) in 1974. To act as their own advertisements, Fortes wanted service area buildings as close to the motorway as possible, and requested prominent light fittings in the cafés so that the warm glow of light would attract customers. (Whether the customers were prepared to turn round at the next junction was another matter). The team that had produced Scratchwood built Corley over abandoned mineworkings and around a footbridge that the Department of Transport had already completed. This ruled out a bridge restaurant, which was the preferred solution of both operator and designers despite the trend towards more restful environments. Sand-coloured fibreglass wall units for the footbridge and parts of the main building were prefabricated and delivered by lorry to be craned into place. Fibreglass offered a durable and lightweight construction material, but its moulding process required easy contours. This accounts for the footbridge looking like a train or aeroplane, and for the voluptuously curved panels above restaurant windows. Bright colours continued inside the building, where pale yellow bricks were set against orange and green furnishings.[36] New designers were brought in for Fleet (M3) - the final service area to be double-sided with an integral bridge - and the single-sided site at Gordano (M5), both opened in 1973. These buildings were based on four adjoining blocks below slated roofs with glass top lights like maltings or oasthouses.[37] When asked to reflect on his approach to the styling of these buildings, architect Issy Spektor commented that 'the early service areas were very mechanical things made of

Above: Corley by night, a beige vision of luxurious motorway service.
Left: Fleet in its 'Scandinavian setting'.
Far left: Detail of Corley.

metal and glass. I thought that when people got out of their car - which was a metal and glass mechanical enclosure - they should go into something completely different. We didn't want to design a pastiche looking like a Swiss chalet, but to use softer, familiar materials - wood and quarry tiles, earthy things. Coming from South Africa, I was very used to light coloured buildings in the sun with the shadows of trees on them. I had an affinity with white concrete blocks and used these for the service areas.'[38] The *Architects' Journal* described the Fleet design as 'restrained and appropriate to the Scandinavian setting'.[39]

Fortes' last service area of the early seventies, and the first one that I can remember visiting, opened in 1974 at Burtonwood on M62 where the motorway passed through bleak terrain that had been negotiated many years before to complete the Liverpool-Manchester Railway. Patrick Gwynne's design, a follow-up to two restaurants he had built for Fortes in Hyde Park, London, during 1963-71,[40] is to me one of the most expressive yet modest and self-contained solutions to the problem of building in a landscape where the road is the only landmark. A bird flying over the site would pass two perfectly octagonal buildings. Behind full-height glass walls, every bit of space was put to use for kitchen, dining areas and offices. On each building a steeple-like form rose up out of the low-set roof. The steeples hid chimneys and

water tanks – there was no direct water supply available for miles around - and were floodlit at night to act as beacons. With the buildings surrounded by grass Gwynne wanted to paint the roofs a conspicuous bright red, but the Royal Fine Art Commission who vetted the design objected to this and copper sheeting was used, which has now weathered to a green colour. For Fortes, Burtonwood proved to be an economic disappointment, as the opening of this portion of M62 coincided with a national recession which impacted heavily on Liverpool, the ultimate western destination of this route.

RoadChef: a new name on the highway

Having won the Killington Lake (M6) site in 1972, Shell-Mex BP needed a caterer to operate the service area. Lindley Catering Investments (LCI) - an entrepreneurial organisation then only three years old, but already active in sports stadia, pubs and restaurants, and operating a chain of Licensed Betting shops - seized the chance to enter the motorway catering business and was soon running the filling station as well. LCI set up RoadChef in partnership with Galleon World Travel. Like Tebay, which is discussed on the following pages, Killington's location offers the motorist an unsurpassable rest stop. Accessed by a long slip road and completely away from the motorway, the site is at the edge of a large reservoir facing towards the Pennines. Resembling an alpine cabin, the single amenity building was constructed from local stone, with a balcony restaurant projecting out from the main block. In form, its design was similar to buildings constructed by the same architects for Ross at Hartshead Moor (M62) around this time.[41] The site was completely redeveloped by RoadChef in 1985.

Above: Patrick Gwynne created a subdued interior for Burtonwood to give motorists a restful break. Ceiling beams were stained dark brown and concealed the lighting units. A mural (not shown) was commissioned for the Grill room.
Right: The original restaurant at Killington Lake, built for southbound travellers on M6 in 1972, and since redeveloped.

Westmorland Motorway Services

Can you feel the difference?

On a hill far from the road, with a view back south of toy-like vehicles on the distant M6, Tebay (West) re-establishes a human scale of operation for roadside refuges. By 1971, when a double-sided service area was being proposed at Tebay for the extension of M6 into Cumbria, the major operators were less enthusiastic about taking on new business. Tebay Junction on the West Coast Main Line railway had recently been closed with many redundancies, and there was some political motivation to create new jobs serving the motorway. When no one tendered for the site, the government had to revise its specification and proposed two smaller, single-sided services (the other area was Killington Lake). John Dunning, a local farmer with experience of the motor trade, saw the opportunity for developing a service area that would benefit the Cumbrian community as

well as motorists. A partnership was formed with the Birkett family, Penrith-based bakers and confectioners. In addition to staking their livelihoods on the venture, Westmorland Motorway Services accepted financial support from Shell Oil. The two families were successful in winning the tender competition for Tebay West. Westmorland would make a virtue out of being the smallest service area operator, using local staff and local products to promote the area. Instructed to capture the essence of a hill farm in traditional materials, Windermere-based architects Stables and Gilchrist[42] designed an amenity building with café, shop and lavatories, and a planted central light well to complete the theme. For increased capacity the buildings were partially redeveloped and extended in 1980 and 1988. A second site operated by Westmorland at Tebay East is described later in this book.

05 Deceleration 1974-1978

A Deserving Case

By 1974 there were 33 motorway service areas in
England, with a further 22 proposed for opening in the
period to 1980. Bev Nutt wrote an article for Design
magazine that reviewed changes in the industry since the
publication of his report in 1967. Nutt felt that his
findings and recommendations of almost seven years
earlier had been little heeded by government, the
operators, or the architects. He restated his view that
financial requirements imposed on caterers restricted
competition and therefore the potential for improvement
in service to motorists, and observed that through better
planning and management, profitability had improved,
but not the food. The government brief for buildings did
little to encourage good design. Nutt speculated on the
role of motorway services, in the light of his forecast that
their future use would increasingly be for rest and
relaxation, and put the case for additional facilities to
include overnight accommodation, picnic areas,
information centres, and rescue service organisation
representation. As in Germany, locally run sites on short-
term leases could give greater flexibility and commitment
to quality. Perhaps the most radical proposal, and one
which ran counter to contemporary thinking on the
supremacy of the car for personal transport, was that

*Whilst breakfast was
being taken, a car
(under three years old -
no MOT certificate
needed) could be
stolen to order in
Milton Keynes, driven
to the service area, and
be sold in Birmingham
before teatime.*

Top: Corley Grill room, about 1976.

service areas close to urban centres should become interchange points for park and ride networks. This would have reduced city congestion by offering large areas of parking for private vehicles by the side of the motorway. It would also have changed the essential nature of the service area as a facility entirely isolated from the wider community - a problem which operators are still addressing today.

The long drag

The oil crisis beginning in 1973 and financial difficulties inherited by the new Labour government of 1974 contributed to a national recession. New service area development was suspended pending the results of an inquiry into the state of their operation, and the industry rumbled on with all the speed of a lorry climbing the incline beyond Watford Gap. Caterers concentrated on maintaining existing business on the main M1, M5 and M6 routes. Customers complained about lack of value for money, and found the standards of food and service were wanting. Operators began to recognise that to attract increased custom, it was better to improve the environment of the service area. At Toddington, Granada pioneered free-flow cafeterias, based on island food counters that removed the need for a single queue, in 1973.

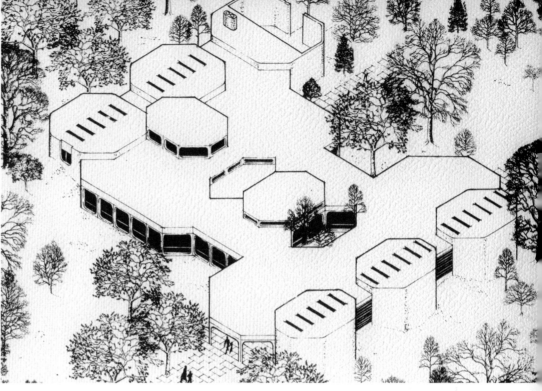

Separate dining areas were merged, and equality for motorway users finally arrived. Concessions for commercial vehicle drivers were maintained by voucher systems for cheaper food. Granada looked to the United States for developments to improve profitability and service, its directors taking a tour of highway and freeway diners and fast food operations. This research was beneficial: Egon Ronay's April 1978 *Survey of Motorway Catering*

Above: Original design for Rownhams (westbound) of 1970, showing the use of several hexagonal units to create a building that would have looked as at home on the moon as in this Hampshire valley.
Opposite page: Vandal-resistant furniture developed by Steelchrome and Bill Finch for Fortes, at Keele (M6) in 1976.

Top: Bothwell M74 (now redeveloped). Designer Tony Cooper comments: 'we were very into black and red in those days'. **Above:** Sandbach, M6, opened as one of the first 'infill' sites to reduce journey intervals between service areas.

attributed most of the improvements in motorway services to Granada.

RoadChef moves ahead

One operator was successful in rapidly increasing its motorway business in the mid-1970s, and contributing some distinctive buildings which for me recapture the spirit (if not the substance) of dynamic design for the uninhibited surroundings of the motorway. From a single successful venture at Killington Lake (M6) in 1972, Galleon RoadChef doubled, and even quadrupled its profits each year between 1972 and 1978, as it built more sites on existing and new routes. Sales of fuel rights to oil companies financed the works.

Tony Cooper, designer of the westbound amenity building at Rownhams and now Development Director at RoadChef,[43] remembers walking through a verdant copse, where now the M27 hurries cars between Portsmouth and Southampton. At a meeting held before construction began, the local planning officer expressed his desire for the tree-filled vista to be preserved, requesting that the service station roof be planted with grass, shrubs and trees. This hanging garden proved too expensive to implement, but rather than obscure the view with a footbridge, a tunnel was provided to link the two

sides. Rownhams was planned in 1970-71, but not opened until 1977. In form the all white building could be said to resemble some kind of moon colony, with several hexagonal pods rising around a food and shopping court enclosed entirely in glass.

Hamilton (M74 northbound) and Bothwell (M74 southbound) of 1975 are two single-sided sites located half a mile apart just south of Glasgow on M74. A scheme offered by the Scottish Development Department failed to attract interest from any service area operators, so the government asked interested parties to make their own proposals. RoadChef got the job. Design was for rapid construction: brick and wood buildings decorated with a mock colonnade of white fibreglass 'tee' pieces (suggesting a comparison with the exterior of Scratchwood - see previous chapter).

Sandbach had been added between Keele and Knutsford as a lorry-only stop on one of the busiest sections of M6. Plans changed and it was opened to all motorway users in 1976. On each side of the carriageways a single square block of smoky glass enclosed the cafeteria, with lower level brick buildings attached on either side of the blocks housing foyer, shop and kitchen areas.

Exterior details were minimal, and the interior a clear space with few columns. Beyond the amenity buildings, free standing water tanks advertised the RoadChef logo. Taunton Deane, which had first been the subject of a tender competition back in 1969, was opened by RoadChef in 1977 (southbound catering only) with the extension of M5 linking the west country with the midlands. When this phase of activity came to an end, RoadChef had rapidly become the third largest service area operator in Britain. They then extended their catering interests to include North Sea oil rigs and 'Roadway Diners' on 'A' roads.

1978: another government inquiry

What really began to liberate service area operators was the so-called 'Prior Report' of 1978, commissioned by the then Labour government (an administration which intended to keep motorway catering under state control) and produced under the chairmanship of Peter J. Prior by the Committee of Inquiry into Motorway Service Areas. Bev Nutt was an official external adviser to this committee. The Committee took a comprehensive look at aspects of activity and use at motorway services and reported on both their poor public perception and how this might be improved by future government policy. The committee noted the paradoxical situation that operators were reluctant to tender for new sites due to poor financial returns, whilst the media asserted that the same companies were making too much money from their activities. It was found that one third of the 38 service areas made a loss, and that overall profits had fallen significantly since the early 1970s. Few caterers were happy about paying up to ten or twenty percent of their takings to the government on top of their site rents, having to provide three types of café and up to five types of fuel, and then being expected to match prices with shops in the town. Although the Prior Report accepted that prices were higher on the motorway than off it, and that food quality was variable, it did not consider profits were excessive, nor the more extreme media criticism valid. It concluded by recording the difficult conditions that operators and their staff endured as a result of the need to cater for widely fluctuating traffic levels, and in the face of sustained vandalism and public abuse.

It seems that the only way for the motoring public to have a better service was for commercial interests to be more fully acknowledged. Even today, in 1999, operators feel that the remaining governmental restrictions prevent them from competing on an equal footing with shops in town.

Above and opposite page: Sandbach when new. This service area became a popular venue for youths meeting up after a night out in Manchester clubs, or when going off to a warehouse party.

A lady used to drive down M6 every week, dressed in pearls and a twin-set. Drove a Jaguar, and back home had a big house and boys at public school. Divorced, she'd fallen on hard times, and to keep the lifestyle going entertained commercial travellers by night at the service area. Select clientele, strictly business. Very nice lady by all accounts.

Simon left college in 1969 and walked straight into a job at a new service station. He remembers the day a lady driver arrived at the petrol forecourt in a small, fast, sports car. Before she was out of the car, a pump attendant had pocketed her petrol cap. 'I couldn't help noticing you've lost your petrol cap, madam . . . I'll see if we have a replacement.' A few minutes and some spit and polish later, a 'new' petrol cap was found and the attendant made a good ten shillings for the weekend.

06 Clearway? 1979-1996

Different scenery

A transformation occurred within the service area industry at the end of the 1970s, and motorists may have noticed a steady improvement in service standards throughout the 1980s as a result of renewed vigour in the activities of the leading operating companies. Competition between operators hotted-up, forcing companies to increase investment and work harder at innovating ideas. Focusing on the appearance of interiors, in-house designers worked with consultants to create higher-quality environments where investment was directed at a sense of comfort and relaxation, rather than resistance to abuse. Growth of trade was so rapid that some buildings only a few years old had to be supplemented by temporary facilities, and then extensively rebuilt. In some cases the designers have struggled to give a consistent overall look to the enlarged premises. On close inspection it is possible to see layers of construction in different materials and styles which give clues to periods of growth like the rings in a tree.

Almost as soon as the Prior Committee's *Inquiry into Motorway Service Areas* was published, a general election brought the Conservatives into power. With the new regime came an intention to sell-off nationally owned

Left: Farthing Corner, M2. Conran Design Associates' work for Top Rank in the late 1970s was characterised by the un-compromising use of toybox colour, softened with beige and off-white. Chairs were bought from an Italian designer. Reconstruction of the buildings has removed this facade.

Designer make-over by Stewart McColl Design for Sandbach, inspired by the clarity and graphics of road signs.

Above: Birch (M62), about 1980.
Opposite page, above: Ferrybridge (M62) 1985.

industries, and the leasing arrangements for service areas fell into this category. Other recommendations of the Prior Report were implemented almost immediately, giving operators some freedom to increase profits, and consequently raise expectations of their own ability to offer motorway users the best possible service. Operators could now make agreements to retail one oil company's products, and so reduce fuel storage, delivery and accounting costs; they could advertise their names and petrol prices on roadside signs. Turnover leases ceased to have effect, removing the high government rents formerly levied on profits. We now take for granted the right to purchase any item at any hour, but twenty years ago legal restrictions on Sunday opening and sales revealed anomalies in goods available at service areas. 'At Corley [visiting Prior Committee members] were told that the shop could sell on Sundays ice cream but not aspirins, lemonade but not a cup from which to drink it, and sponges but not sanitary towels'.[44] Important details for motorway users included the introduction of children's play spaces (remember those giant boot-shaped 'Wendy' houses and smiling tree climbing frames?), and showers for lorry drivers to save them washing-down at a sink in the toilets.

Several small operators remained on the motorway, hanging onto a few sites that had been developed some years previously. Alan Pond Group, Kenning, Mobil, Ross and Top Rank each contributed a particular style of service that would be erased by company amalgamations during the late 1980s and early 1990s.

Go Granada

Much of the development in this period is recorded in Granada's own newspaper *Grapevine*, which noted every success and change in the organisation. From ten motorway sites in 1977, when Trusthouse Forte were close behind with nine service areas and Rank and RoadChef in equal third place with five each, Granada expanded rapidly. Kinross services (M90) had been purchased in 1982, Burton West (M6) was leased from Mobil Oil in 1983 (Mobil's other operation at Michaelwood, M5, went to Ross Services) and Ferrybridge (A1M) opened in 1985. Situated at the intersection of key east-west (M62) and north-south (A1M) routes, Ferrybridge was notable for being the first motorway service area developed entirely through private enterprise – now standard practice in the industry. Its opening also came at the end of a major strike by miners, and many of the original staff were miner's wives.

Architecturally, the amenity building was distinguished by its striking triangular form. With the structure based on an 'a'-shaped frame, it was effectively all roof, and the interior free of internal columns so that it was easier to adapt for future changes. Opening profits at Ferrybridge were immediately double the expected levels; besides private and commercial vehicles, 180 coach loads a week were being fed. In 1986 the lease for Monmouth (A4) was taken on by Granada, and Chieveley built in an 'area of outstanding natural beauty' just off the M4. Stirling (M9/M80) opened in 1986 and Blyth (A1M/A614) the year after. Seven trunk road ('A'-road) sites were also added for 1988, with 43 service areas as Granada's goal to be achieved by 1992. Once the Department of Transport permitted overnight stays at service areas, operators were able to build public accommodation on previously redundant land within the perimeter of sites. Stirling was the location for Granada's first 'lodge hotel' in 1986, soon motorway lodges were available all over the country.

Granada's building and refurbishment programme saw that key sites were redeveloped, drawing on trends in the 'High Street' rather than the motorway environment. If these concepts proved

profitable and were received favourably by customers, then the makeovers were extended to other sites. Based on the model of shopping centres such as Brent Cross, planning moved towards open foyer spaces, often under a glass roof, surrounded by catering, retail and amusement outlets. In the restyled restaurants and 'food courts' counters could be differentiated by individually-styled 'shopfronts', and identified to the customers through colour-coding and large signs – when you've come in from some hours of driving at 70mph, you expect service to be as simple and fast as the motorway. Granada commented that their 'Carving Tables', introduced in 1983 to serve roast meat dishes, were unique on the motorway, and helped to distance dining from the image of convenience foods (for some years Heston enjoyed a regular trade from local drivers out for Sunday lunch). At the same time Granada's own brand 'Burger Express' operation was becoming an increasingly significant profit earner. Fortes began to transfer catering methods and themes from the relatively easy-going environment of their department store cafés, coffee shops and park restaurants to the motorway services.

The separate transport café was no longer required – one service could feed all. Now-familiar own

brands emerging during this period included the 'Country Kitchen' (Granada), 'Granary' (Trusthouse Forte) and 'Orchard's' (RoadChef) self-service restaurants. As the decade progressed, the sophistication of interior design increased. Colour scheme trends can be plotted against changes in the 'Habitat' catalogues of the day: red, black and grey ('high tech'); red, blue and yellow ('bold primary colours'); yellow and green ('natural, soothing'), and mauve, pink, blue and beige ('new pastels'). All these combinations were set against exposed wood, melamine and sprinklings of granite and polished brass. Carpets

and fabrics for seating tended towards geometric patterns in contrasting colours, not unlike the textiles once used for car interiors (there were limits imposed by the availability of sufficiently durable materials). After the regimented rows of seats installed during the 1960s and 1970s for cost and security reasons, individual booths were reinstated to create more intimate dining areas. Some designers also turned back to the past to make restaurants appear wholesome and more customer friendly, introducing details like reproduction Victorian lamp standards, artificial plants and imitation leaded windows.

Countrified

From the mid-1980s, subject to pressure from local authority planners and environmental groups, design of new buildings for service areas began to follow the trend of the out-of-town supermarket shed. Large structural shells with clear internal spaces like warehouses were styled to imitate the idealised image of rural vernacular architecture: brick walls, tiled roofs and rustic details. Killington Lake (M6 southbound), completely rebuilt by RoadChef in 1985, is a good example of traditional materials being used appropriately for the location. For M25, the London Orbital Motorway, services would be located at the four compass points. Sites were allocated to avoid a monopoly situation. In the south, RoadChef won Clacket Lane. Granada gained Thurrock in the east (completed 1991), and Welcome Break[45] (the new name for Trusthouse Forte motorway catering) got the South Mimms site on the northern arc of the motorway. A decision could not be reached about the western service area, and there are still long gaps for travellers leaving M4 to travel east.

RoadChef's Clacket Lane service area between Junctions 5 and 6 of M25, commenced full operation in July 1993, with racing driver Damon Hill making a celebrity appearance. The architecture could be compared to a modern interpretation of the country manor, set in carefully planned areas of tree-planting to imitate the surrounding woodland and screen parking areas. In the entrance foyer of the amenity buildings, bay windows were arranged to suggest individual shop fronts. A bronze fountain sculpture by William Pye named 'Flyover' was the central feature of the westbound mall. Large areas of window give direct visual connection between the restaurants and landscape.

Above: Killington Lake (M6), 1985.
Right: Clacket Lane (M25), 1993. Using local materials, buildings were designed to represent the 'Gateway to Surrey' (westbound side), and 'Gateway to Kent' (eastbound side). At Clacket Lane travellers from the continent may gain their first glimpses of modern English vernacular architecture.
Opposite page left: A Trusthouse Forte washroom after redesign, 1979.
Opposite page right: Chieveley (M4), 1990.

Thurrock, Granada's services on M25 near the Dartford Tunnel. Walkways over a dry 'moat' connect parking areas with the glass entrance atrium. A Travelodge forms part of the main building.

Perhaps it is the isolation of service areas, or their proximity to long-established (and influential) settlements, that made this trend for looking back appropriate. It is clear that the motorist is most concerned about the standard of service inside the building, and that in the operators' eyes the success of the design rests on flexibility and ease of use. Catering and retail concepts have a working life of perhaps five years before changes in the market require a new concept to be introduced. In a shed-like structure, it is a simple matter to reconfigure the whole interior rapidly without extensive disruption to business. By openly imitating agricultural buildings, this aesthetic hides behind the suggestion that the service area is part of the pre-motorway environment, that progress has come full circle and gone back to the land. I would also suggest that it is as anonymous as the less distinguished products of 1960s modernist architecture – with the brick box simply made bigger and decorated with the past, rather than the future, in mind. Through the 1980s, the particular nature of the service area that had been modelled on the roadside cafeteria began to evaporate in favour of a more universal experience of consumption. I have to acknowledge my own nostalgia for the 1970s and a past phase of Englishness. It may have been tacky, it could be poor quality, but I can't help wondering if there wasn't something strangely special about the motorway culture that we have now lost.

Changing vehicles

Government proposals for deregulation of service area provision into the private sector were the subject of a consultation document published by the Department of Transport in February 1992. This was the first time in the short history of service on the motorway that relaxation of central control had been countenanced and it would effectively change the conditions for their construction and operation. One of the reasons cited for reducing the restrictions were the gaps in services on M25 and M4, and the need for increasingly large sites at the standard 25-30 mile interval to cope with predicted traffic growth. Deregulation took place in August 1992. The Department claimed that operators intended to maintain the site's full 24-hour service, picnic areas and shopping. Statutory powers governing signage, access roads and the requirement that only non-alcohol drinks be available, are still held by the government. Site freeholds were sold off in 1996. Clauses in government agreements preventing service areas becoming destinations in their own right, deterred potential purchasers. Operators had to bid against other businesses and non-motorway interests bought some sites. Where this situation arose the

Victorian pub windows for the extended restaurant at Knutsford, 1994.

Department of Transport leases remain in place until 2030. Until deregulation, the government obtained planning permission. Now this arduous and expensive task has become the responsibility of the operators. Consents for new on-line (on motorway) service areas are extremely difficult to obtain from local authorities, and schemes are likely to meet opposition from local residents and amenity groups. This has had the effect of promoting service area construction on A-class trunk roads and, coupled with the near saturation of the industry, this seems to be where most operators favour future developments.

Led by Michael Guthrie (who had worked for Mecca when Trowell was built in 1967), Pavilion Services bought the Top Rank sites in 1992 and rapidly refurbished facilities using a strong brand image. It was Pavilion that applied their corporate colours of green and yellow to the service area buildings at Knutsford, Aust and Forton. Pavilion lasted but a short time, being acquired by Granada in 1995. Granada was successful in its battle for Forte plc in January 1996, gaining control of the Welcome Break service areas, Travelodges, Little Chef and Happy Eater restaurants. As a result of the near

monopoly resulting from this merger, Granada undertook to dispose of the former Welcome Break sites, and these were purchased by Investcorp of Bahrain, with Michael Guthrie as adviser. Kenning Services (now operating only the Strensham M5 site) was bought out by management in November 1994 and became Take a Break. A year later Blue Boar was bought out by its management. After some negotiation with Granada and Welcome Break, Blue Boar and Take a Break were sold to RoadChef in 1998, and RoadChef itself was then acquired by Japanese bank Nikko Europe plc.

Opposite page: Westmorland is a location not a brand: having operated a single-sided site at Tebay (West), since 1972, Westmorland Motorway Services decided to expand their activities on the other side of motorway M6. Tebay East opened in 1993 to serve southbound traffic. Built in limestone using traditional methods, and with roof timbers reclaimed from defunct textile mills in Lancashire, this amenity building is one of the few new service area developments that can honestly and favourably be compared to vernacular architecture. The scale of the building - it houses a large foyer, shop, WCs and four dining areas - is kept at a modest scale by the low-set walls, unfussy details and the presence of a water garden across which visitors can view moorland and mountains. From the building, footbridges span the water to picnic areas, and these are very popular in good weather. Tebay East is the only service area to have won a Civic Trust Award.

Left: Only 24 miles from Blackpool (take the M55), disco meets Victoriana at Forton, 1994.

Opposite page: In the film Butterfly Kiss (Dan Films,1996, directed by Michael Winterbottom), the sociopath Eunice (Amanda Plummer) seeks her lost friend Judith. Eunice is joined in her unsuccessful quest by filling station assistant Miriam (Saskia Reeves) and the pair drift around the roads of north-west England, attempting to escape but going nowhere. To emphasise the emptiness and endless qualities of this existence the filmmakers chose service areas for some of the locations - an unglamorous and rarely depicted aspect of the British landscape.

Left: Photographer Martin Parr has made regular visits to service stations, places he finds good for the observation of all human life. This picture is from the mid-1980s.

07 Refreshment to retail 1997-2000+

A different gear

Cars are now designed for sustained high-speed operation and increased levels of comfort, so that the need for a series of journey stops is significantly reduced. Long-distance coaches provide refreshments and toilets on-board, and only make stops for legally required driver rest breaks. To maintain and increase the facilities and profits, operators have widened the available range of services, including a range of food choices, mini shopping malls, business centres and now internet cafés. In this way the service area once again parallels the airport: it is a place of transient occupation for the motorist, who has the opportunity for rest, but is also distracted from the process of travel by food and shopping.

Little towns by the roadside

Located on the brow of a hill and visible over some distance to northbound travellers on M1, Donington Park could be compared with the Romantic tradition of English architecture: it is at once both art and monument, dominating and welcoming.

One development route is to follow the example of airports. Granada, which employs 6000 staff and has 120 million customers a year, wanted to 'find out what [service areas] offer you, what they do with your life…we wanted to offer a stop of choice.'[46] Its market research supported the vision of Managing Director Maurice Kelly that airports were widely seen as a positive part of the travel experience. Mini-malls had been trialled at Trowell (M1) and Tamworth (M42) during 1998; now Granada set

out to provide service areas of the future that were like 'an airport or little town beside the road'.

Donington Park, opened on 8 July 1999 at Junction 23a on M1, represents Granada's first opportunity to invest all their best ideas in an entirely new site. Development of service areas as destinations - places that people drive to, rather than through - is still opposed by the government on the grounds that it would increase traffic overcrowding at junctions and slip roads. Granada makes it clear that Donington Park is aimed at convenient express shopping for the commuter motorist, and would not wish it to be a destination even if this were permitted by regulations. It can be said that this scheme brings together the convenience of shopping found in an airport terminal, with a service for motorists. I would compare this approach with the example of decentralised retail centres developed over the last half-century in North America, to serve commuters and out-of-town shoppers.[47] In this way, the idea of village blurs commercial activity with traditional definitions.

The 'tray-slide' type café is disappearing. Catering revenues increase significantly when a Quick Service Restaurant (QSR) is opened. Motorists seem to want food that can be identified by pointing to an image on the menu, and then have it placed in their hand. This also suits the British tradition of consuming food in the private car or coach, rather than sharing space with strangers. Own-brand catering now operates alongside franchised fast-food chains. Brand franchisees have found this recognition of product a good solution to the problem of food quality that has beset service areas for many years.[48] It also allows for more centralised distribution, and higher profits on food sales from a smaller floor area, freeing-up space for other retail activities. Granada wants to become 'the home of brands on the motorway'. Whereas the service area shop was originally no more than a kiosk for consumables and souvenirs, products are now merchandised by familiar high street brand names: Sock Shop, Thornton's Chocolates, Tandy Express, Knickerbox and others.

Many motorists do not go beyond the fuel forecourt for their needs. Once a greasy refuge for petrol pump attendants selling car spares and sweets, the design of forecourt buildings is evolving rapidly. Of much increased size, and with better use made of the available space, shops at the newer service areas can offer a full off-peak catering service. Commuters can now have their photographs processed or dry cleaning done during the day and collect it on the way home.

Below: Forecourt shop at Donington Park.
Opposite, main picture: Interior of Donington Park at night.

Top: London Gateway
(formerly Scratchwood, M1),
after refurbishment by
Welcome Break.

Fuel sales have become a smaller proportion of the total possible income from the forecourt.

Welcome Break

During 1997 and 1998 Welcome Break has invested £120 million in refurbishment of service area facilities. Extended foyer spaces, new toilet, restaurant and shopping areas have given somewhat run-down sites such as Newport Pagnell, Charnock Richard and Woodall much-needed improvements. Architects and designers for these works have been J. Ward Associates. A trademark feature of the redeveloped buildings is the wave-form canopy roof over entrances. Grey metal panels hide old walls behind sheer surfaces, and large areas of glass fill the new foyer spaces with light. It has been said that even a few steps will discourage a significant proportion of travellers from using service area amenities; an important practical feature is Welcome Break's introduction of escalators at buildings with more than one storey. By night details of the roof lines are highlighted with blue neon strips prompting comparisons with the decoration aesthetic of multi-screen cinemas.

Oxford (Wheatley) is a single-sided site accessed from Junction 8 on M40, the Oxford-London motorway. Breaking away from the separation of services into different rooms, here the concourse and food court is a single uninterrupted space below an aluminium sheet roof which carries on over the perimeter wall and water channel as a sunscreen supported on steel columns. This lightweight canopy is made of the same material as the roof of Sir Norman Foster's transport interchange for North Greenwich Jubilee Line station at the Millennium Dome in London. Food outlets and a shop occupy two edges of a single free seating area.

Hopwood Park, on M42 south of Birmingham, is larger than its exterior would suggest, and contains a mezzanine floor over the food court. In design terms it is less distinguished than Oxford, but the grounds include fountains and rest areas for motorists to escape from the bustle of the building, where a designer goods shop competes with the usual retail outlet and 'Game Zone' for customers' attention. The availability of open areas which can be physically occupied by travellers, rather than just viewed from a restaurant, is an increasingly necessary factor of service area design.

RoadChef is currently working on plans for a new site at Winchester (M3) to be opened in 2000.

Welcome Break has recently opened two new sites which demonstrate their commitment to innovation in service area design. This is Oxford (M40).

'Live Aid Day 1985. He was married. I was living with my boyfriend. He had shoulder length hair. I still had the vestiges of New Romantic frills. The problem: how to fix a secret meeting which would hide behind my trip to my mum and dad in Cheshire and his to see his old college mate in Coventry. The venue: Woodall Services on the M1, south east of Sheffield. It's just before that point where the trucks veer off onto the M18 on the way to Scotland. It was heavy with midsummer coming and going. Me in a white Spitfire. Him, unsexily, in a red Fiesta. Well he was married. Two nervous journeys. Will she, won't she? Will he, won't he? He did, I did. But who'd have noticed, in amongst those Sierras and Cavaliers, the DAFS and Scanias, that something known to no-one was happening amid the hordes? We know the facilities that most services are judged on. The cleanliness of the loos. The temperature of the food. The price of the petrol. Do the handbooks ever say if there's a wood nearby where in summer there's a bed of dry leaves as soft as any duvet? Perhaps they should. I'm sure we're not the only ones for whom Woodall Southbound is part of the lexicon of love.'

On the way to becoming a place

'We must recognise that the roads and streets and alleys can no longer be identified solely with movement from one place to another. Increasingly they are the scene of work and leisure and social intercourse and excitement. Indeed they have often become the last resort for privacy and solitude and contact with nature. Roads no longer merely lead to places; they are places'.[49]

As the first of several radial highways, M1 cut through the landscape with the single governmental objective of getting motorists from where they were to somewhere else. The locality ceased to exist; the road seemingly to go on forever. The British landscape became a panorama to be observed at speed and without identification. Do service areas contribute to this loss of local distinctiveness? In the present sense of England, does it matter that Toddington is in Bedfordshire, Newport Pagnell in Buckinghamshire or Watford Gap in Warwickshire?

Service areas are seen as things that exist on the way from one place to another. Along with other transport buildings, they are increasingly experienced more as transit halls, non-places, than real sites of history. Service areas are regarded primarily for their function, which is to meet the imperatives of long-distance terrestrial travel by road vehicle - relief and refreshment. But they are places in themselves, in that they use space, form part of the topography and are thus landmarks, and affect their environment and motorists.

When the first service areas opened in this country they presented a novelty not unlike that of cinemas some three decades earlier. I would not suggest that all service areas were architecturally as accomplished as the floodlit, neon-bathed art deco confections that appeared on high streets and arterial roads across the country before World War Two, but there was a similar spirit of modernity, progress and dynamism associated with the motorway that invited attention and participation. In moving away from the more exuberant designs of the mid-1960s, the architectural products of the early 1970s might be criticized for their lack of character. They were examples of giving precedence to flexible planning and circulation, and in this they met their purpose well and with some modesty. Now service areas are shopping malls and food courts. Again like airports, these are private spaces with a public purpose, places to process people quickly and efficiently. But paradoxically the designers must give consideration to making these places comfortable for motorists so that a longer stay is encouraged. In doing this, the idea of place is constantly reinvented by architects, interior designers and branding consultants. This is an ephemeral and ever-changing micro-landscape, of shuffling spaces and scene-shifting.

But architecture is only part of the place-making. It is the movement and assembly of people which creates meaningful sense of place. Whilst the average stop for a motorist is twenty minutes outside the personalised space of the car, service areas have communities of staff who occupy them all day, and by choice or circumstance remain with an operator for years; they may even see further generations of their family take employment at the same service area. For them, personal histories are attached to their own careers, that of their colleagues, and the many levels of encounter with motorists. Here the received account of Britain's motorways is transformed into personal stories, which loop and meander around the buildings themselves. History happens here too.

In the rear view mirror

The first service area schemes were produced with little prior research, planned without consideration for future expansion potential, and basic in their construction. Several of the earlier service station buildings were experiments in how far mass concrete and prefabricated walling could be taken in the expression of modern transport architecture and design, right in the middle of a new faster Britain. Stifled by government, abused by some of the customers and much of the media, they deteriorated into places that might relieve urgent need, but were unlikely to do much else. During the mid-1960s there were one or two attempts to provide an architectural response equal to the new highways. By the end of the decade enthusiasm on the part of operators and road users had waned and it took a government-commissioned inquiry and a new generation of architects, to rethink service area design. The caterers that provided the full English breakfasts, and the people designing the buildings to serve them in, tried to evolve facilities in which they could trade efficiently. Buildings became simple boxes for the necessary services, sometimes distinguished by an unusual roof, but otherwise doing their best not to be noticed at all. In the late 1970s, after the worst of the football hooligans had vanished in the distance, and restrictive practices had been partially lifted, the service area became a relatively sophisticated enterprise.

Like other buildings that inadvertently became tourist attractions for their symbolic modernity, service areas acquired history quickly. From glamorous beginnings a large number of sites, on an ever-increasing road network, provided the motorist with a variable experience of catering in the context of modern design. Growth of the industry slowed in the mid 1970s as first the oil crisis and then financial difficulties came to bear upon the motorway construction programme. Around 1978 the appearance of the service area became increasingly influenced by local authority guidelines concerning the visual impact of buildings. A desire on the part of the operators to produce attractive and flexible structures, resulted in all-purpose 'sheds' styled with pastiche rural motifs. The 1990s have seen diversification in design as part of a strategy to improve services, the public's perception of motorway service areas, and of course to maximise profits. Significant advances have been made to the standard of facilities, and in the architectural expression of what different agencies consider to be appropriate for this building type. While leases remain in place, the operators' obligations to provide twenty four hour services to motorists are fixed. When site leases expire in 2030, there is the potential for service areas to close or change in line with the interests of the freeholder. Some service areas off the main motorway routes return low profits. Were an operator to default on its agreement to provide government-stipulated services, then the signs advising drivers of an approaching service area would be removed from the motorway. Slip roads could be closed, and the site redeveloped for other uses. Will these road transport buildings become redundant in the way that structures for canals and railways ceased to be used? Could this be part of a British motor archaeology? Perhaps a constant factor is the customer. As long as family cars and excursion coaches use the motorways, service areas remain part of our travelling lives. Beyond 'tea and a pee', they offer a place to observe and participate in the highly designed experience that travel has become.

Ways ahead

Motorway service area operators have a tradition of working both together and in competition. Rather than offer a single conclusion to this story, it seemed appropriate to ask the present companies for their own views on new directions in roadside services.

Granada

Granada Road Services' vision of the future is born out of the overwhelming desire to fundamentally change the customer's perception of motorway service areas - not with hype but with a genuinely different offering that gives travellers places to stop because they want to, not because they have to. Inspired by the sophistication of the airport style experience, the Granada MSAs of the future will be "towns by the roadside", bringing travellers the choice, quality and above all the credibility of well-known high street brands on the motorway. 'Best brands, best choice" is not just a marketing strapline, it's a philosophy that is sustained through strong partnerships with recognised brands throughout our estate including catering, retail and forecourt. Supported by comprehensive research identifying who our customers are and what they want, Donington Park is the realisation of this vision. It is not just revolutionary in its design but also in its execution. The idea of 'zoning' ensures that each of our customer segments is catered for: the forecourt enables the commuter to do some top-up shopping, drop in their dry-cleaning or get their holiday snaps developed. The main amenity building houses state-of-the-art baby changing facilities and children's play areas as well as the mini retail malls and numerous branded, catering outlets. The business user will find their needs catered for by Travelodge at present, with new and innovative facilities soon to be introduced.

The motorway network is at a critical juncture in the services it can offer and the expectation of the public. The cost of entry into this restricted industry requires substantial capital to be available. Motorway services are currently seen as a distress stop, and the Highways Agency has discouraged a product offer that does not meet that simple benchmark. The public is changing its expectations and buying requirements. There is now a political move towards consumerism and an orchestrated approach to competitive pricing. The catering and main shop offer is the primary source of profitability for the operator, with premium prices to pay for the infrastructure of 24-hour service required by the government. Operators must balance the income from a more interesting shopping experience with the capital cost and the political pressure to price service areas in line with High Streets, but High Streets do not carry the same cost base as service areas, and are not limited in the offer that they can provide to the consumer. RoadChef would like to see complete freedom of offer to the traveller, who can be encouraged to stop for an hour or more, to sit and eat and consume wine if they are not driving. There are plenty of suggestions that motorway services should be more like airports and railway stations. If motorway services are to survive and not become uncompetitive in the face of developments at roundabouts off motorways, they will have to become more flexible and price competitive than at present. The government has therefore got to release the sector from the 40-year-old restrictive policies and allow it to compete with the total travellers market.

Welcome Break prides itself on offering the best break available for travellers on British motorways. This quality promise is delivered in four ways, through better choice and availability of food; a better and more relaxing environment; better levels of customer service; better value for money. Wecome Break is currently upgrading all its facilities in the UK as part of a £150 million development programme. Existing sites are being improved - 23 new Burger Kings, 15 KFCs and 12 La Brioche Dorees have been introduced in the last year alone - and new ones developed. Key among these is Hopwood Park, Welcome Break's new state of the art service area at Junction 2 of the M42. This development includes a 35 acre nature reserve where visitors can stroll and relax, as well as more mainstream facilites including: a food court with Burger King, La Brioche Doree and Granary Express outlets; a café and restaurant overlooking the nature reserve; a children's play area; a convenience store; a discount designer clothes store; fountains and a terrace. As UK planning regulations restrict further expansion of motorway service areas, the development opportunity is focussed on locations off motorway (on trunk roads) or within other travel related areas such as railway stations and airports. Welcome Break aims to be the UK's leading provider of services to travellers, and will open its first off motorway service area near Derby in 2000. As integration with Europe progresses and cross-border travel becomes easier, Welcome Break will work to position its "Better Break" proposition at the head of traveller services continent wide.

Westmorland

As a small family business operating at one location, it is not surprising that Westmorland has a rather different point of view to that of the three major corporate motorway service operators. Its policy is to provide a better quality of catering by producing as much as possible in-house, using local produce where possible, with competitive prices. it is individual in its style, celebrating the attractions of Lakeland culture, and rejoicing in being a 'one off' which attracts its own clientele. Unlike its competition, Westmorland has eschewed the 'brand' route, making instead a very individual offer of quality and style.

The hope of the government on privatisation had been to see a variety of services develop which would offer a wide range of choice to the customer and competition within the industry. Instead there has been consolidation into three groups which now offer a broadly similar choice of branded products.

There seems little immediate scope for more small operators on the motorway. The growing choice in fast food brands will be followed by a more varied range of retail opportunities. Off-motorway facilities will become more important in meeting a growing market not covered by the current choice, but new development on the motorway will be rare. Westmorland will continue to plough its lonely furrow, making up for its inability to market nationally by trying harder and offering better value.

FIRST
Motorway Services

The future of motorway service areas in the next millennium.

The MSA business of the future will continue to be dominated by the three major operators, although providing they are able to differentiate their offer, the independents will survive.

Brands both catering, and retail will continue to feature strongly, and in particular Granada will use retail brands to drive market share.

Pressure on the operators to maintain a competitive pricing policy, could lead to a relaxation on the current destination rules, and allow more 'commercial' uses of the whole MSA site.

By 2002 the last of the new MSA locations will be agreed, and the MSA estate will reach maturity.

First Motorway Services currently operates at Magor (M4), Bolton West (M61) and Bridgwater (M5).

From 1983 to 1992, Timothy lived by sleeping only in motorway service stations, travelling back and forth across the Midlands and north of England.[50]

Gazetteer

This list includes the majority of service areas developed in the period 1959-1999. Some sites have been omitted where they conform to an established pattern of design rather than an innovation (for example the several neo-vernacular schemes of the mid-1980s to early 1990s).

		opened	original operator	architect	present operator	comments
M1	Scratchwood	1969	F	GCBA	WB	now 'London Gateway'
	Toddington	1965	G	CHE	G	
	Newport Pagnell	1959	MS	SCS	WB	
	Watford Gap	1959	BB	HWW	RC	
	Leicester Forest East	1966	B	HVL	WB	
	Donington Park	1999	G	BM	G	
	Trowell	1967	Me	KN	G	
	Woodall	1968	F	RG	WB	
A1(M)	Woolley Edge	1972	E	CFST	G	
	Washington-Birtley	1970	E	CFST	G	
M2	South Mimms	1999	WB	JWA	WB	redeveloped 1999
	Farthing Corner	1963	TR	SCS	G	now 'Medway'
M23	Rownhams	1977	RC	KA	RC	
M25	Thurrock	1991	G	SBT	RC	
	Clacket Lane	1993	RC	DM	WB	
M3	Fleet	1973	F	BDA	RC	
	Winchester	2000	RC	TDP	G	opening 2000
M4	Heston	1968	G	JAR	G	redeveloped 1983/1996
	Chieveley	1986	G	EPR	G	
	Membury	1972	R	HVL	WB	
	Leigh Delamere	1972	R	CPDH	G	
	Aust	1966	TR	RHL	G	now 'Severn View', M48
M40	Cherwell Valley	1994	G	SBT	WB	
	Oxford	1998	WB	JWA	WB	
M42	Hopwood Park	1999	WB	JWA	G	
	Tamworth	1990	G	SBT	G	
M5	Exeter	1977	G	HVL	G	
	Gordano	1973	F	BDA	G	
	Michaelwood	1971	Mo	M	WB	
	Strensham	1963	K	TPB	RC	
	Frankley	1966	G	HVL	G	
M6	Corley	1972	F	GCBA	WB	redeveloped 1994
	Hilton Park	1970	TR	TPB	G	
	Stafford (Northbound)	1996	G	BM	G	
	Keele	1963	F	TVA	WB	
	Sandbach	1976	RC	KA	RC	
	Knutsford	1963	TR	SCS	G	
	Charnock Richard	1963	F	TVA	WB	
	Forton	1965	TR	TPB	G	
	Burton in Kendal	1970	Mo	M	G	
	Killington Lake	1972	RC	HVL	RC	
	Tebay West	1972	W	SG	W	
	Tebay East	1993	W	UJP	W	
	Southwaite	1972	E	CPDH	G	southbound opened 1977
M61	Rivington	1971	K	TP	FMS	opened as Anderton
M62	Burtonwood	1974	F	PG	WB	
	Birch	1972	E	CFST	G	
	Hartshead Moor	1973	R	HVL	WB	
	Ferrybridge	1985	G	FJ	G	
M74	Annandale Water	1993	BB	PP	RC	redeveloped 1987
	Hamilton/Bothwell	1974	RC	KA	RC	redeveloped 1987
M8	Harthill	1971	APG	not known	RC	

Key to architects: BDA: Building Design Associates; BM: Broadway Malyan; CFST: Challen Floyd Slaski Todd; CHE: C.H.Elsom & Partners; CPDH: Castle Park Dean Hook; DM: Dancey & Meredith; EPR: EPR Partnership; FJ: Fletcher Joseph; GCBA: Garnett Cloughley Blakemore & Associates; HVL: Howard V. Lobb & Partners; HWW: Harry W. Weedon & Partners; JAR: James A. Roberts; JWA: J Ward Associates; KA: Kinnair Associates; KN: Kett & Neve; M: Mobil's in-house architects; PG: Patrick Gwynne; PP: Parr Partnership; RG: Riley & Glanfield; RHL: Russell Hodgson & Leigh; SBT: Scott Brownrigg & Turner; SCS: Sydney Clough, Son & Partners; SG: Stables & Gilchrist; TDP: Turnkey Design Partnership; TPB: T.P.Bennett & Son; TVA: Terence Verity Associates; UJP: Unwin Jones Partnership.

Key to operators: APG: Alan Pond Group; BB: Blue Boar; E: Esso; F: Fortes; FMS: First Motorway Services; G: Granada; K: Kenning; Me: Mecca Leisure Group; Mo: Mobil Oil; MS: Motorway Services (Fortes & Blue Star Petroleum); R: Ross; RC: RoadChef; TR: Top Rank; W: Westmorland; WB: Welcome Break.

Notes to the text

1 Thomas Burke (1947) *English Inns*. London: Collins.
2 See Anon. (1962) 'The motorway to the Sun', *Concrete Quarterly*, January-March (52): 6-14.
3 W.R.Thomson (1963) 'Institute of Highway Engineers: Motorways in Worcestershire', *Traffic Engineering & Control*, 5 (2): 101.
4 P.R.V.Hammond - Partner, Weedon Partnership - in a letter to the author, 25 November 1998. Harry W. Weedon and Partners were better known for their cinema design work; prior to Watford Gap the firm had built filling stations for Blue Boar.
5 Bill Finch, former Development Director for Fortes motorway division, interviewed by the author, 24 April 1999.
6 For a comment on the original American bridge restaurants see Daniel J. Boorstin (1962) *The Image: Or What Happened to the American Dream*. Harmondsworth: Penguin Books: 121.
7 Anon. (1967) 'Motorway service area, Leicester Forest East, M1 Motorway', *Building*, 213 (6491): 128.
8 Anon. (1970) 'Motorway Restaurant on the M1', *Interior Design*, (June): 358.
9 Lance Wright (1972) 'Food, Petrol but no joy', *Architectural Review*, 151 (904): 379.
10 Anon. (1967) 'M6 Motorport', *Interior Design*, (November): 56.
11 Ibid.
12 Anon. (1968) Mecca Village: At your service Round the Clock. [Publicity leaflet].
13 The murals were sketched by Gordon Burrell, brother in law of Eric Neve, the architect for Trowell. From an interview with the author, 4 April 1999.
14 James A. Roberts is better known for his work on the redevelopment of Birmingham Bull Ring area and the St. John Centre, Liverpool.
15 Anon. (1968) 'Service station for the inner man', *Sunday Times*, (7 January).
16 After Aust (M4, now M48), Scratchwood was the first single-sided service area. Its situation away from the motorway, accessed by long slip roads, would become a standard pattern for service areas developed from the late 1970s.
17 The external concrete frame, and the articulation of beam-column joint with stainless steel elements, had been used by Skidmore, Owings and Merrill for certain projects of the mid-1960s.
18 Richard Burnett, architect for Scratchwood, interviewed by the author, 15 December 1998.
19 Anon. (1964) 'Keeping the Motorway Away', *Architects' Journal*, 149 (25): 1614.
20 Anthony M. Perry (1968) 'Motorway Services', *Financial Times*, (22 June).
21 Frederick Steyn (of Challen Floyd Slaski Todd), interviewed by the author, 24 November 1998.
22 Brian Gatensbury (former Managing Director, Granada Motorways), interviewed by the author, 26 November 1998.
23 Ian Breach (1972) 'Design on the Motorway', *Design*, 288 (January): 45.
24 Bev Nutt (1967) 'Motorway Catering', *Service World International*, I (6): SW28.
25 Bev Nutt, ibid.
26 Granada Motorway Services policy statement, 10 June 1968.
27 Challen Floyd Slaski Todd were appointed for the first Esso projects, and recommended Castle Park Dean Hook (CPDH) as a second practice for the work. Bev Nutt, main author of the 1967 research report on motorway services, was directly involved in planning meetings with CPDH, and the Southwaite and Leigh Delamere schemes incorporate features proposed by Nutt.
28 Frederick Steyn commissioned Louise Grose after seeing her poster design for London Transport.
29 Steyn, ibid.
30 Steyn, ibid.
31 Lance Wright (1972) 'Food, Petrol but no joy', *Architectural Review*, 151 (904): 384.
32 Christopher Dean proposed the pyramids, and they were engineered by Tony Hunt.
33 A feature recalled by Tom Jestico, then a junior architect for Leigh Delamere, in a telephone interview with the author, 13 September 1999.
34 Michael Boyle, former Managing Director of Ross Motorway Services, interviewed by the author, 29 August 1999.
35 Lance Wright (1975) 'Motorway Service Area, Membury, Berkshire', *Architectural Review* 158 (942): 100.
36 The high specification of this project prompted Fortes to seek other architects for future service area work.
37 Fleet and Gordano seem to owe much both formally and materially to Louis Kahn's Trenton Jewish Community Center of 1955-56.
38 Architect Issy Spektor, interviewed by the author, 23 November 1998.
39 Sam Lambert (1973) 'Signpost for Services', *Architects' Journal* 158 (50): 1434-1436.
40 All three projects used polygonal plans to create unusual building forms.
41 Originally a Scandinavian building detail, the dominant sloping roof feature was much used in North America from the 1950s.
42 Architect Gordon Stables had designed a scheme for the Burton West service area, which was to be developed by a private consortium. This project failed to materialise but Stables was retained by Westmorland Motorway Services.
43 Tony Cooper worked with Jack Kinnair on the design of RoadChef service areas. When Kinnair died, Cooper was asked to join the RoadChef management.
44 Peter J. Prior et. al. (1978) *Report of the Committee of Inquiry into Motorway Service Areas*. London: HMSO: 15.
45 In order to distance their high-quality hotels from the motorway business, Fortes retained the trading name Welcome Break for all their service areas.
46 Granada Road Services Managing Director Maurice Kelly, 25 June 1999.
47 For a detailed discussion of out of town shopping centres see Richard Longstreth (1998) *City Center to Regional Mall*. Cambridge (Mass.): MIT Press.
48 The origins of branded fast food marketing in North America are discussed in Paul Hirshorn and Steven Izenour (1969) *White Towers*. Cambridge (Mass.): MIT Press.
49 J.B.Jackson (1994) *A sense of place, a sense of time.*. New Haven: Yale University Press.
50 Court report by John Dodd, *ES Magazine*, 2 July 1999.

Bibliography

Anon. (1959) 'Curbs on Motorway Garages', *Sunday Times*, (20 September).

Anon. (1970) 'Esso Motor Hotels', *Interior Design*, (September): 569.

Augé, Marc [translated by John Howe]. (1995) *Non-Places: introduction to an anthropology of supermodernity*. London and New York: Verso.

Barker, Paul. (1999) 'In praise of suburbia', *Blueprint*, (March): 28-32.

The Bartlett School of Architecture, University College London. (13 January 1978) *Motorway Service Area research in 1966 by The Bartlett School of Architecture, University College London. Recommendations to the Ministry of Transport*. London: The Bartlett School of Architecture, University College London.

British Travel Association. (12 March 1968) *The British on holiday: Summary of regular surveys of British holidaymakers 1951-1967*. London: British Travel Association.

Butterfly Kiss. (1996). Written by Frank Cottrell Boyce, directed by Michael Winterbottom, produced by Julie Baines.

Catterall, Claire [ed]. (1999) *Food: Design and Culture*. London: Laurence King Publishing in association with Glasgow 1999 Festival Company.

Charlesworth, George. (1984) *A History of British Motorways*. London: Thomas Telford.

Croft, Catherine [ed]. (1999) *On the Road: the art of engineering in the car age*. London: The Architecture Foundation and Hayward Gallery Publishing.

Crowe, Sylvia. (1960) *The Landscape of Roads*. London: The Architectural Press.

Cruickshank, Dan. (April 1996) 'Forton Services M6, Lancashire.' *RIBA Journal*: 49-55.

Drake, James, H. L. Yeadon and D. I. Evans. (1969) *Motorways*. London: Faber and Faber.

Fairbrother, Nan. (1970) *New Lives, New Landscapes*. London: The Architecture Press.

Graham, Paul. (1983) *A1 The Great North Road*. Bristol: Grey Editions.

Holland, Harry. (1971) *Travellers' Architecture*. London: George G. Harrap & Co.

Horwitz, Richard P. (1985) *The Strip: an American place*. Lincoln: University of Nebraska Press.

Jakle, John A, and Keith A. Sculle. (1994) *The Gas Station in America*. Baltimore: The John Hopkins University Press.

Hobson, Dorothy. (1982) *Crossroads: The Drama of a Soap Opera*. London: Methuen.

Koch, Alexander. (1959) *Restaurants Cafés Bars*. Stuttgart: Verlagsanstalt Alexander Koch.

Liebs, Chester H. (first paperback edition, 1995) *Main Street to Miracle Mile: American Roadside Architecture*. Baltimore: The John Hopkins University Press.

Lohof, Bruce A. (1974) 'The Service Station in America: The evolution of a Vernacular Form', *Industrial Archaeology*, 11 (2): 1-13.

Maxwell, Robert. (1972) *New British Architecture*. London: Thames & Hudson.

McKenna & Co. (1992) *Deregulation of Motorway Service Areas*. London: McKenna & Co.

Miller, Daniel, Peter Jackson, Nigel Thrift, Beverley Holbrook and Michael Rowlands. (1998) *Shopping, Place and Identity*. London: Routledge.

Nuttall, Jeff and Rodick Carmichael. (1977) *Common Factors/Vulgar Factions*. London: Routledge & Kegan Paul.

Rais, Guy. (1969) 'M1 sandwiches and queues for tea upset MPs', *Sunday Times* (17 March).

Ritter, Paul. (1964) *Planning for Man and Motor*. Oxford: Pergamon Press.

Smith, Michael A., Stanley Parker and Cyril S. Smith [eds]. (1973) *Leisure and Society in Britain*. London: Allen Lane.

Starkie, David. (1982) *The Motorway Age: Road and Traffic Policies in Post-war Britain*. Oxford: Pergamon Press.

Ward, Colin and Dennis Hardy [commissioned and edited by Alexandrine Press, Oxford]. (1986) *Goodnight Campers!: The History of the British Holiday Camp*. London: Mansell Publishing.

Witzel, Michael Karl. (1992) *The American Gas Station: History and Folklore of the Gas station in American Car Culture*. Osceola (Wisconsin): Motorbooks International.

Zukin, Sharon. (1991) *Landscapes of Power: From Detroit to Disney World*. Berkeley: University of California Press.

Index